Pelican Books

Britain in Figures: A Handbook of Social Statistics

Alan F. Sillitoe was educated at a Quaker school – Saffron
Walden – and after working in London for two years as a
hospital porter he read sociology at Nottingham University.
He worked in town planning for two years, and since then
has been teaching sociology. His present post is Senior
Lecturer in Sociology at the University of London, Gold-
smith's College. He has a special interest in urban sociology,
and has broadcast and lectured in this field. Alan F. Sillitoe
is married, and lives in Hampstead.

GW00514792

Britain in Figures A Handbook of
Social Statistics

Alan F. Sillitoe

Second Edition

Penguin Books

Penguin Books Ltd, Harmondsworth, Middlesex, England
Penguin Books Inc., 7110 Ambassador Road, Baltimore, Maryland 21207, U.S.A.
Penguin Books Australia Ltd, Ringwood, Victoria, Australia

First published 1971
Second edition 1973
Copyright © Alan F. Sillitoe, 1971, 1973

Made and printed in Great Britain by Butler & Tanner Ltd, Frome and London
Set in Monotype Times

Typography by Norman Ball
Diagrams designed and illustrated by The Penguin Education Illustration Department
Film for the grid backgrounds of graphs was supplied by H. W. Peel & Co., Ltd, Middlesex

Contents

Part II Social

Part III Education

Introduction

The aim of this book is to make available, to the student or the general reader, a selection of statistics showing social trends in this country during the last twenty or thirty years.

Criticism during recent years of government statistics may, at a very sophisticated level, be justified, but at a more general level the fact is that Britain is lavishly endowed with statistical material. The difficulty for many of us is that we may not know in which reports or publications to look, or, even if we do, they may not be easily available. This may be as true for the undergraduate student who requires documentary evidence for an essay as for the everyday reader who wishes to use the resources of his local library to settle a disputed point in an argument.

The second edition of *Britain in Figures*, while updating the statistics themselves, aims as far as possible to follow the contents and range of material presented in the first edition. This ensures the continuity which is such an important feature of any factual reference book.

The basic principle of the book is that selected statistical series are presented in graph, diagram or chart form. On the page facing the illustration is a commentary giving any further information needed to understand the statistics themselves. Often this takes the form of definitions of the various items shown, as well as additional facts and figures.

The span of years selected as the basic module for the book is the period from 1935 to the present day. Thus it is possible to make a comparison (which in some cases can be very instructive) with the pre-war period, as well as to see the impact which the war years had upon social trends.

Ideally perhaps, this time span would be used for all the graphs. But in many cases the data simply do not permit this. The material in this book is heavily dependent upon government publications and statistical sources, and often these go back only to the post-war period, or the basis for the statistics has been changed. In the case of education, much of the present school and college system dates from the 1944 Education Act, and the GCE dates from the early 1950s.

In other cases, a longer time series has been chosen deliberately. A graph showing population change or birth rates only since 1935 would reveal little of interest. The real changes had occurred earlier, in the late nineteenth century or the early part of this century. Again, statistics covering trade unions or labour relations in the 1960s need the perspective provided by figures showing the struggles of the 1890s and the 1920s. So, where necessary, the time series starts at an earlier date.

Just as the time sequence used for the different graphs varies, so too does the coverage of the four constituent countries of the United Kingdom. Wherever possible UK figures have been used, and for this purpose the Annual Abstract of Statistics proves invaluable. But in some areas of social life the four countries have agreed to differ to the extent that their statistics are simply not comparable. The most obvious examples of this are in the fields of education and the judicial system.

At various points in the book a comparison is drawn, usually in a bar graph, between the experience of Britain and of other countries. This is done, not to indulge for its own sake in the sport of providing international 'league tables', but because in many cases (for example in labour relations) we need the comparisons in order to see our own situation in perspective. Occasionally, such comparisons can have the power to shock, or surprise, as when they dispel some time-honoured maxim like 'India is the most densely-populated country in the world,' or 'Britain is the most heavily-taxed nation in Europe.'

The choice of countries for these diagrams is partly dictated by the available statistics, and partly by the need to compare like with like, to examine a range of countries in a similar economic and industrial position to our own.

Government departments are at the receiving end of a constant flow of information and statistics. When the deadline for a Monthly Digest or an Annual Abstract approaches, figures must be published which are the latest currently available. Later information may make them subject to revision. Economic statistics in particular seem to suffer (or should it be benefit?) from this process, and figures in this book incorporate revisions of earlier published statistics, as no doubt they in their turn will be revised in the years to come.

Whether in their revised or unrevised versions, statistics can often conceal as much as they reveal. Crime statistics are notorious for this. Figures are catalogued under the heading of the offence committed, and if this offence comes to be viewed less seriously by society, and the penalty lightened, it may be moved from one part of the classification and placed in another, with a consequent jump in the statistics. Again, the number of 'persons found guilty' may depend on the efficiency of the police, or upon the readiness of the public to report a particular piece of behaviour to the authorities.

Religious statistics must also be viewed with caution. They tell us how many people belong to the Churches, but they do not tell us how many of them go to church. Still less are they able to point to the 'strength of religion', or the place held by religious belief in people's hearts and minds.

One final point must be made with some force. This is not a sociology book. The love–hate relationship between sociology and statistical data has continued for nearly a century, and has not ended. But it is rare for an *explanatory* model of people's behaviour to be made from facts and figures alone. This book does not seek to interpret *why* people no longer go to the cinema, or why they take part in industrial disputes, although it is unlikely that one could understand these things without at least *some* factual knowledge. But the facts do not speak for themselves.

Part I
Population

Population growth
Births
Deaths
Illegitimacy
Expectation of Life
Population density
Immigration

Population Growth

Overall size of population: United Kingdom

The graph shows how the population has grown since the very beginning of the nineteenth century. The figures are for the United Kingdom as it is now, so for the period before the partition of Ireland they include only that part of Ireland which is now north of the border.

The commencing date for this graph, 1801, was the year in which the first national census was carried out. Since then a census has been conducted every ten years, with the exception of 1941. This does not mean, however, that we have no knowledge of population size during the centuries before 1801. During the sixteenth and seventeenth centuries a number of *estimates* were made by contemporary writers, and these have been used by present-day scholars to build up a picture of early population size. For instance, William Farr (a nineteenth-century statistician and census official) estimated that the population of England and Wales had been 6·1 million in 1700, and 6·3 million in 1750.

Similar estimates suggest that the population at the time of the Norman invasion was 1·5 million, and that it must have increased at the rate of approximately one million per century until the period shown in our graph. From then onwards, the rate of growth became dramatic, and by the middle of the century the population had doubled in size.

Obviously, the overall size of the population will be determined by a number of factors, the most important ones being the rate of births and deaths, and we must turn to these in order to find an explanation of the trends shown in this graph.

Source:
Census Reports

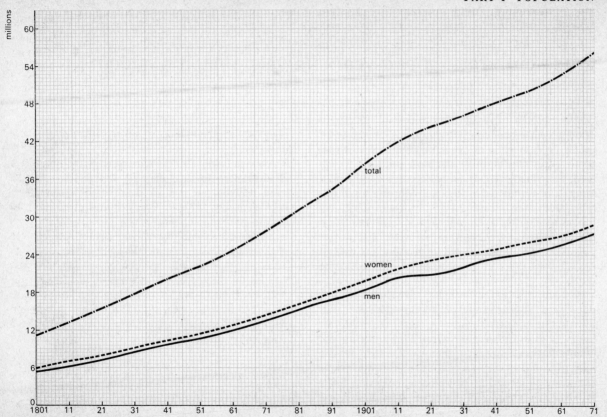

millions

total

women

men

1801 11 21 31 41 51 61 71 81 91 1901 11 21 31 41 51 61 71

Fertility

Crude birth-rate, at two-year intervals: United Kingdom

The crude birth-rate, like the corresponding measure for deaths, is the number of live births expressed as a proportion (per thousand) of the total population in a given year. The term 'crude' reflects the fact that as a measure of *fertility* the birth-rate is a far from sophisticated index. Any measure which calculates something (in this case births) as a proportion of total population will be affected by changes in the overall size of this population. Other more elaborate measures are used to calculate the eventual implications of changes in the number of *births per married woman*.

But with this caution in mind, the crude birth-rate does show the general trend of fertility since the latter part of the nineteenth century, when the birth-rate began to fall. The precise causes of this decline are elusive. It is associated, in a general way, with increasing industrialization, urbanization, improvements in the social and legal status of women, and rising living standards. But the way in which these factors work, and their relative importance, is still a matter for scholarly debate.

Average family size, as a measure of the number of children born to each married woman, has declined from between five and six children for couples who married in the 1870s to a little over two children for couples marrying in recent years.

At the same time, the gap in family size between white-collar workers and manual workers has narrowed. The traditional pattern was broadly one where fertility was low at the top of the social scale and high at the bottom. This pattern survives, but in a less extreme form, and there are clear signs that the rise in post-war fertility was greatest among the families of middle-class and professional workers.

Source:
Annual Abstract of Statistics

Fertility

Crude birth-rates: International

This is the first diagram in which the 'base' of the vertical scale does not start at zero. This is intentional, and has the effect of 'exaggerating' the extent of differences between countries. However much the birth-rates of various countries differ, they all operate roughly within the same range, although a few countries (e.g. Mexico) have birth-rates a good deal higher than those shown here. These figures are for 1970.

Not all countries keep sufficiently sophisticated records for strict international comparisons, and the UN Statistical Office, which calculates these figures, confines them to countries for which the data are comparable. Birth-rates in industrialized countries tend to be lower than elsewhere, and the same trends in fertility can be observed in the recent history of most of the western nations. High fertility in the nineteenth century was followed by declining birth-rates until the inter-war period, and in turn by a period of higher fertility during the 1950s and early 1960s. The latest development has been a downturn in fertility, dating in many of the countries shown opposite from around the mid 1960s. According to recent reports by the Institut National d'Études Démographiques in Paris, the birth-rate has now fallen below the replacement rate in Denmark, Finland, West Germany, Holland, Italy, Sweden, Hungary and Czechoslovakia. In Hungary the low birth-rate is now seen as something of a national problem, and measures to counteract it have been recommended which are similar to those advocated in Britain during the 1930s.

Source:
UN: Population and Vital Statistics Report

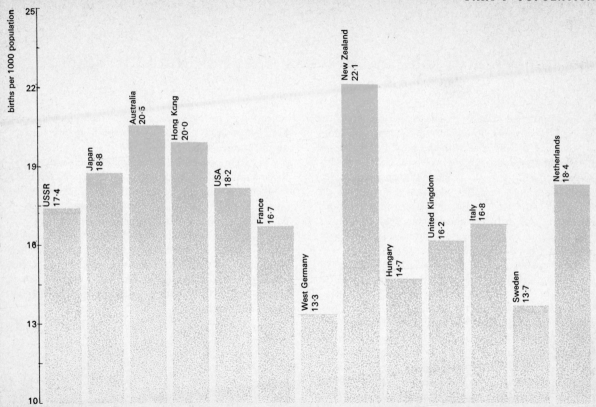

births per 1000 population

USSR 17·4
Japan 18·8
Australia 20·5
Hong Kong 20·0
USA 18·2
France 16·7
West Germany 13·3
New Zealand 22·1
Hungary 14·7
United Kingdom 16·2
Italy 16·8
Sweden 13·7
Netherlands 18·4

Illegitimacy

Illegitimate birth-rate, at ten-year intervals: United Kingdom

Ten-year intervals have been chosen here in order to permit a time-span long enough to compare late nineteenth-century experience with the present. One result of this is to 'iron out' short-term fluctuations in illegitimacy rates, and there was in fact just such a short-term rise between 1940 and 1945 which does not appear on the graph. In 1945 the rate for England and Wales reached a peak of over nine, largely because couples who in normal circumstances would have married were prevented from doing so by the war.

The illegitimacy rate, or ratio, is the number of illegitimate births expressed as a percentage of all live births.

High illegitimacy rates in Scotland during the nineteenth century were usually a feature of rural life. Rates were high in the villages and low in the towns, and the steady depopulation of rural Scotland must be seen as the likely explanation for the decline in the rate. Migration can affect the figures in another way: it is possible that the declining rate for Northern Ireland may be a reflection of people's desire to seek the anonymity of a big city (possibly London or Liverpool) for the birth of an unexpected baby.

The recent post-1960 rising trend in illegitimacy seems to be characteristic of different social groups from the 'old' nineteenth-century rates. The trend started in the cities, especially in London and the South, has been commoner among unmarried than married women, and has been more a feature of middle-class life than was the case earlier in the century. Generalizations of this order can be made from the available statistics but judgements about changes in social and moral conduct cannot be made without a much more sophisticated study of the evidence.

Source:
Annual Abstract of Statistics

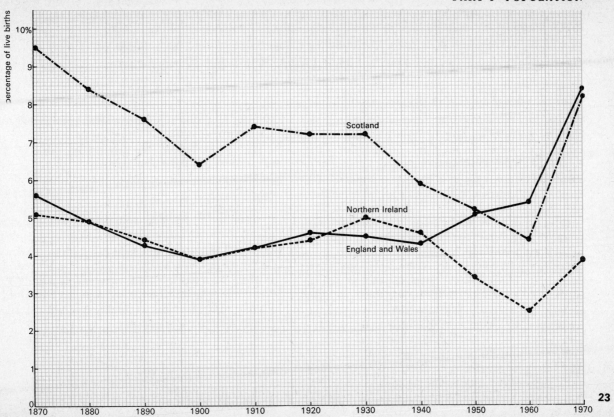

Age

Age distribution of the population: United Kingdom

The demographic device of the 'population pyramid' is basically a simple bar graph which has been raised vertically to give a 'profile' of the age structure of the population. If the same scale is used to compare two countries, or (as is the case here) two centuries, the shape of the pyramids will show at a glance any differences between the two.

Three periods have been chosen for comparison: the census of 1871, figures for 1971, and official projections for the year 2000.

The late nineteenth century, with its high birth- and death-rates, shows a heavy preponderance of young people in the population. By the middle of the twentieth century, this tendency had been eliminated, and the result was a population more 'balanced' in terms of age distribution.

By the end of the century the 'pyramid' shape will have largely re-asserted itself. Successive years of (by 1930s standards) higher fertility in the second half of the century will mean large numbers of children, followed by gradually smaller numbers of middle-aged and elderly people.

The balance between the numbers of people in the labour force and those who are dependants (young and old) has, in fact, become slightly *more* favourable since the 1870s.

The forecast for the year 2000 is one made by the Government Actuary's department, and is contained in *Population Projections 1970–2010* (HMSO), published in 1971. Forecasts of this kind for the year 2000, or for later dates, vary very much according to the time at which the forecast is made. Recent (i.e. early 1970s) projections have scaled down the expected turn-of-the-century population size, as fertility has declined from its high level in the early 1960s.

Sources:
Census Reports
Annual Abstract of Statistics

1871 census

Age	women	men
over 80	100,000	70,000
75–79	120,000	100,000
70–74	220,000	190,000
65–69	290,000	280,000
60–64	410,000	360,000
55–59	450,000	410,000
50–54	600,000	550,000
45–49	650,000	600,000
40–44	770,000	700,000
35–39	840,000	760,000
30–34	980,000	890,000
25–29	1,130,000	1,000,000
20–24	1,270,000	1,140,000
15–19	1,340,000	1,320,000
10–14	1,460,000	1,490,000
5–9	1,630,000	1,630,000
under 5	1,840,000	1,850,000

millions 4 3 2 1 0 1 2 3 4 — women men

1971 census

Age	women	men
over 80	887,000	362,000
75–79	841,000	442,000
70–74	1,224,000	767,000
65–69	1,504,000	1,186,000
60–64	1,695,000	1,488,000
55–59	1,737,000	1,608,000
50–54	1,682,000	1,597,000
45–49	1,776,000	1,736,000
40–44	1,661,000	1,656,000
35–39	1,567,000	1,600,000
30–34	1,605,000	1,660,000
25–29	1,831,000	1,884,000
20–24	2,115,000	2,172,000
15–19	1,897,000	1,998,000
10–14	2,073,000	2,189,000
5–9	2,297,000	2,418,000
under 5	2,203,000	2,319,000

millions 4 3 2 1 0 1 2 3 4 — women men

2000 forecast

Age	women	men
over 80	1,265,000	497,000
75–79	1,122,000	661,000
70–74	1,235,000	908,000
65–69	1,323,000	1,160,000
60–64	1,440,000	1,369,000
55–59	1,617,000	1,595,000
50–54	1,993,000	2,014,000
45–49	1,814,000	1,851,000
40–44	1,983,000	2,038,000
35–39	2,292,000	2,365,000
30–34	2,240,000	2,305,000
25–29	2,291,000	2,350,000
20–24	2,414,000	2,478,000
15–19	2,466,000	2,559,000
10–14	2,572,000	2,699,000
5–9	2,665,000	2,806,000
under 5	2,749,000	2,904,000

millions 4 3 2 1 0 1 2 3 4 — women men

Deaths

Crude death-rate, at two-year intervals: United Kingdom

Birth- and death-rates were both high in the nineteenth century, and here we see the fall in the death-rate during the period in which this decline took place – mainly between the turn of the century and the inter-war period.

The 'crude death-rate' is the number of deaths as a proportion (per thousand) of the total population in a given year. Throughout this period official statistics give figures for *civilian* deaths only, and so do not take account of the approximately three quarters of a million members of the armed forces killed between 1914 and 1918, and 300,000 killed from 1939 to 1945.

The 'peak' in the death-rate at the end of the first world war was caused by the world-wide epidemic of influenza.

The causes for this long-term decline in mortality are many, and it is difficult to allocate their relative importance. During the second half of the nineteenth century working conditions (especially for women and children) improved, and sanitary reform attempted to curb the spread of epidemic and infectious diseases. Recent research suggests that the most important contribution to rising health standards in this period was the overall rise in living standards, and especially in diet, which reduced people's vulnerability to killer diseases like tuberculosis and typhus. Improvements in medical techniques made a much smaller contribution in the late nineteenth and early twentieth centuries than is generally realized.

Source:
Annual Abstract of Statistics

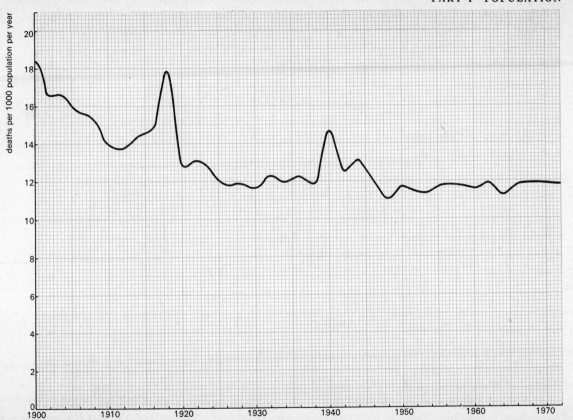

Deaths

Crude death-rates: International

These comparisons, which are for 1970, are again based upon calculations made by the UN Statistical Office from returns made by the member countries.

In a particular country, changes in death-rates over time are a useful though not complete guide to changing health conditions. When one country is compared with another, this principle holds good in general terms, but in certain cases can be very misleading. As death-rates are calculated as a proportion of the total population, the age structure of that population is a vital part of the equation. A country which, for example, was populated only by elderly people, would have a very high death-rate because its population was all in the age-group in which death occurs most often. Thus in real life, when a country has a 'balanced' age structure with a large number of middle-aged and elderly people (see page 25), it will tend to have a higher death-rate than a country in which, whatever the health conditions, there is a predominantly youthful population. The most obvious case in point is Hong Kong, which has a more 'youthful' population than countries like France, Germany, or the United Kingdom.

So far as the advanced industrial countries are concerned, there is not much scope left for reductions in mortality, and any reductions in the future are likely to depend as much on changes in people's behaviour (smoking, diet, road deaths) as upon broad-based social policy in areas like housing and health.

Source:
UN: Population and Vital Statistics Report

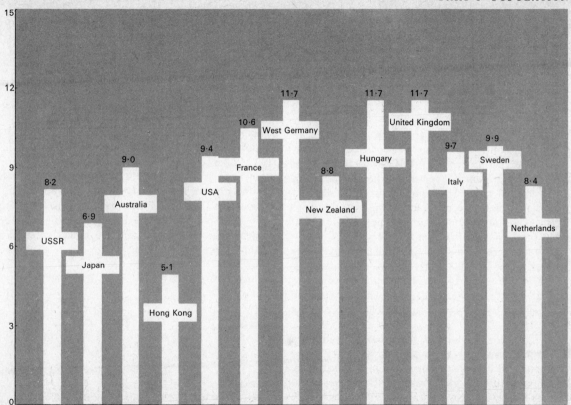

deaths per 1000 population

15

12

9

6

3

0

USSR 8·2
Japan 6·9
Australia 9·0
Hong Kong 5·1
USA 9·4
France 10·6
West Germany 11·7
New Zealand 8·8
Hungary 11·7
United Kingdom 11·7
Italy 9·7
Sweden 9·9
Netherlands 8·4

Expectation of Life

Average life expectation at birth: England and Wales

Another, and certainly more graphic, way of expressing changing death-rates is to look at people's expectation of life. Technically speaking, this means the average number of years which they would expect to live, from given dates of birth. The bottom axis in the diagram opposite is for the year of birth, so clearly the more recent figures involve predictions. People born in 1930 or 1960 have not yet lived out their life-span.

Like all averages, the average for life expectation is the result of both high and low figures. The average for the 1870s was affected by the large numbers who died in infancy or childbirth, so a person who had survived to the age of, say, 30, would have been likely on average to live longer than 40 or 42.

As the figures on page 33 show, baby boys have a higher infant mortality rate than girls. Later in life they are more prone to suffer death in war, in road accidents, and in accidents at work. In retirement, women are still physically less vulnerable, and the 'gap' between the life expectation for men and women has remained proportionately the same since the 1870s.

At the very top of the age-scale, there has been little increase in the proportion of elderly people who reach ninety or one hundred. *Very* old age is not much more common than it was a century ago; the main change in this period is that a steadily increasing number of people are living to attain the biblical prediction of three score years and ten.

Source:
Registrar General's Annual Statistical Review

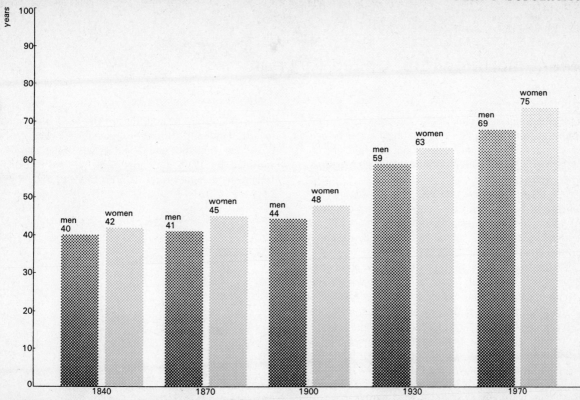

Infant Deaths

Infant mortality rate: United Kingdom

The infant mortality rate, unlike the crude death-rate, is a measure of death as a proportion *of a specific age-group*. Deaths of infants under one year old are expressed as a proportion (per thousand) of all live births in a given year.

The infant mortality rate was high throughout the nineteenth century, and no doubt in earlier centuries. At 150 to the thousand in 1870 it meant that 15%, or roughly one in seven of all babies born, failed to survive to their first birthday.

The pattern of infant mortality during the child's first year of life shows that over six of the deaths (per thousand) occur during the first day, over four occur during the remainder of the first week of life, just under two between one week and four weeks, and six deaths occur during the other eleven months of this first year.

The infant mortality rate has always been higher for boys than for girls; in 1971 the rate was 20·2 for males, and 15·5 for females. At the beginning, as at the end of their lives, males prove to be the least hardy.

It is interesting to note that in the 1870s the figures for Scotland and Northern Ireland were well below those for England and Wales. This difference had vanished by 1910, and now Scotland and Northern Ireland have higher rates than do England and Wales.

Source:
Annual Abstract of Statistics

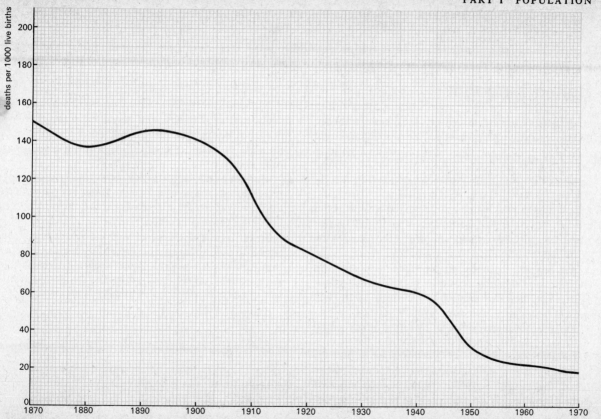

Regional Change

Percentage growth in standard regions, 1901–71: United Kingdom

Since the early part of this century, the country has been divided into a number of standard regions, and these are used here to show the shifts in population which have occurred since 1901. The figures show the percentage growth of the population of each region, with a comparison for Scotland and Northern Ireland.

In this period the boundaries of the regions have been altered, the most recent change being in 1965 when 'new' standard regions were adopted as the basis for the government's economic planning policy.

The *new* standard regions have been used for this diagram, and the growth in their populations is calculated as if they had existed continuously, with their present boundaries, ever since 1901.

As a commentary on the changing geographical pattern of population since the beginning of the century, a regional comparison such as this is only partially successful. It can show *growth*, but not the extent to which this is due to *mobility*. What does reveal itself clearly, however, is the continued growth of the Mid-lands and of London and the South-east. London itself has *declined* in this period, but London is surrounded by counties in which population growth has been steady.

This long-term shift in population is, in a sense, a return to the position held before the industrial revolution, and before the nineteenth-century growth of the industrial towns and cities.

So far as the last decade is concerned, it would be wrong to talk about a 'drift to the South-east'. Migration (rather than natural increase) during recent years has favoured mainly East Anglia and the South-west.

Source:
Census Reports

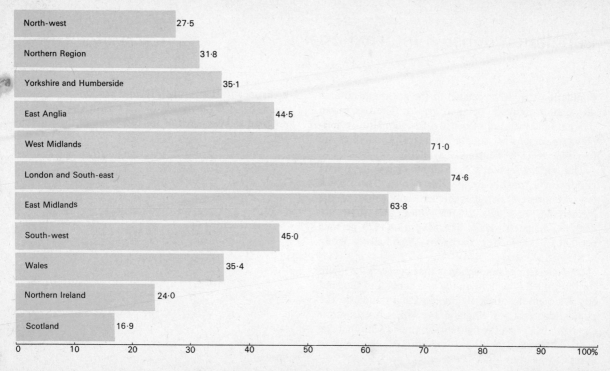

North-west 27·5

Northern Region 31·8

Yorkshire and Humberside 35·1

East Anglia 44·5

West Midlands 71·0

London and South-east 74·6

East Midlands 63·8

South-west 45·0

Wales 35·4

Northern Ireland 24·0

Scotland 16·9

0 10 20 30 40 50 60 70 80 90 100%

percentage growth **35**

Density

Population density: International

Population size, when related to the geographical area of a country, gives population *density*. The recognized international measure of density, for comparative purposes, is persons per square kilometre. The figures are for 1969, the latest currently available.

The countries chosen here show variations among nations of a roughly comparable nature. There are a few instances of densities higher than those of the Netherlands or England and Wales, and these are densely populated islands like Mauritius (428 persons per square kilometre), Barbados (589), Hong Kong (3,859) or Monaco (15,436)!

One interesting comparison is that between the figure for the United Kingdom on the one hand, and England and Wales on the other. By international standards, the population density of England and Wales is exceptionally high, but when the figure is combined with that for Scotland (66) and Northern Ireland (107) the result is a less conspicuous total.

The Netherlands shows a sharply reduced figure compared to that in the previous edition of this book; this is because previously Dutch inland waters were not counted as being part of the total area of the country.

Source:
United Nations Statistical Yearbook

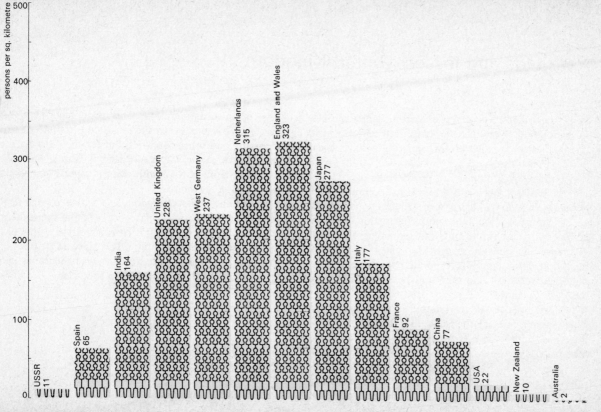

persons per sq. kilometre

USSR 11 · Spain 65 · India 164 · United Kingdom 228 · West Germany 237 · Netherlands 315 · England and Wales 323 · Japan 277 · Italy 177 · France 92 · China 77 · USA 22 · New Zealand 10 · Australia 2

37

Migration

Net gains and losses: United Kingdom

It is important to appreciate that a figure for *net* migration only shows the balance (plus or minus) which remains when the figures for emigration have been matched against those for immigration in a given period. The actual numbers of people entering or leaving the country during the nineteenth century were never counted, so the figure for net migration is arrived at by comparing the total of births within a given period with that for deaths, and assuming that any difference not thus accounted for must be due to migration. These figures incorporate revisions of earlier published statistics, and may well be revised again in the years to come.

Two main waves of migration are discernible, one which occurred during the 1880s, and the second which took place during the first twenty years of this century. Most of the people who left went to countries within what was then the Empire.

No census was conducted in 1941, because of the war, but the overall figure for 1931–51 suggests a strong flow of inward migration. This is in fact what did happen. To a small extent it consisted of refugees from Germany and other countries, but for the most part it consisted of earlier waves of British migrants who were returning from abroad with their prospects ruined by the world depression.

Within the United Kingdom as a whole, a great deal of ebb and flow takes place between the constituent countries. For Scotland and Northern Ireland this has meant continuous net outflow ever since 1871, but for England and Wales it has meant a considerable net *inflow*, since 1931, from these two countries.

Sources:
Census Reports
Annual Abstract of Statistics

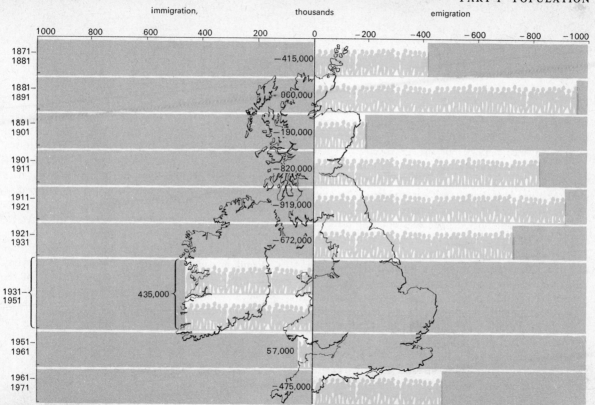

immigration,   thousands   emigration

	1000	800	600	400	200	0	− 200	− 400	− 600	− 800	− 1000

1871–1881   −415,000

1881–1891   −000,000

1891–1901   −190,000

1901–1911   −820,000

1911–1921   −919,000

1921–1931   −672,000

1931–1951   435,000

1951–1961   57,000

1961–1971   −475,000

Immigration

Commonwealth and foreign-born population

The outcome of the last fifteen years of Commonwealth immigration is partly revealed by the figures published in the Advance Analysis of the 1971 census. These totals refer to country of birth, so they include migrants who have come to this country within their own lifetime, and would not include their children who have been born and brought up in Britain.

The figures also include people from countries, as the 1971 census puts it, 'whose descent was not native to those countries'. An example would be where children were born in India or Pakistan while their parents were working in the colonial service. Again, it would include children born to British occupying forces in Germany.

So as a picture of the impact of immigration this information is necessarily somewhat incomplete. Ideally, it would be supplemented by statistics showing the pattern of flow from all the Commonwealth countries; in practice this is not possible. The figures for immigration from 1962 onwards are relatively complete for all countries, and include statistics published under the provisions of the 1962 Commonwealth Immigrants Act, as well as from the International Passenger Survey. But figures before 1962 include Home Office estimates, and are incomplete so far as Australia, New Zealand and Canada are concerned.

In the diagram, Pakistan includes what is now Bangladesh, and the 'Old Commonwealth' refers to Australia, Canada and New Zealand. As a proportion of the population, the total born outside Britain (3·3 million people) constitutes 5·6%; the 'new Commonwealth' total is 1,157,000, which is 2·1% of the British population, and as can be seen the largest single contingent is from the Irish Republic (1·3% of the total population).

Source:
1971 Census

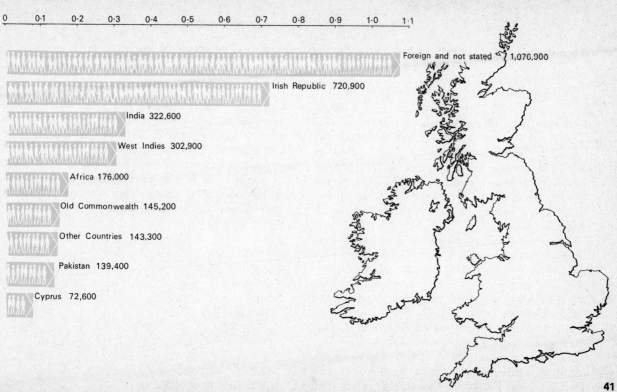

millions

0   0·1   0·2   0·3   0·4   0·5   0·6   0·7   0·8   0·9   1·0   1·1

Foreign and not stated   1,070,900

Irish Republic 720,900

India 322,600

West Indies 302,900

Africa 176,000

Old Commonwealth 145,200

Other Countries 143,300

Pakistan 139,400

Cyprus 72,600

Immigration

Registered aliens by country of origin: United Kingdom

The somewhat unfriendly term 'aliens' is the official description given to persons who are neither United Kingdom citizens nor British subjects, and who have not taken out British citizenship. Aliens must be 'registered' with the police, but since 1961 this requirement has only been imposed upon aliens who are not normally resident in this country. This change has had the effect of reducing by two thirds the number of registered aliens.

Among aliens who are not required to register (and therefore not shown in the figures opposite) are children under sixteen, NATO or Commonwealth soldiers on duty here, foreign diplomatic and consular officials, and visitors who spend less than three months in the United Kingdom.

South Africans became registerable in 1963, after South Africa had left the Commonwealth.

The countries listed are the ones from which the largest contingents of aliens came in 1971. The total of all aliens was 194,000, of whom 104,000 came from European countries, 14,000 were from Africa, 38,000 from the North American continent, 34,000 from Asia and 700 from the USSR. There is even a category of 500 persons of 'nationality uncertain'.

One of the more interesting changes in recent years is the rise in the number of people from Japan resident in this country. From a modest total of 870 in 1960, the number has increased to 1,500 in 1965 and to 4,900 in 1971.

Source:
Annual Abstract of Statistics

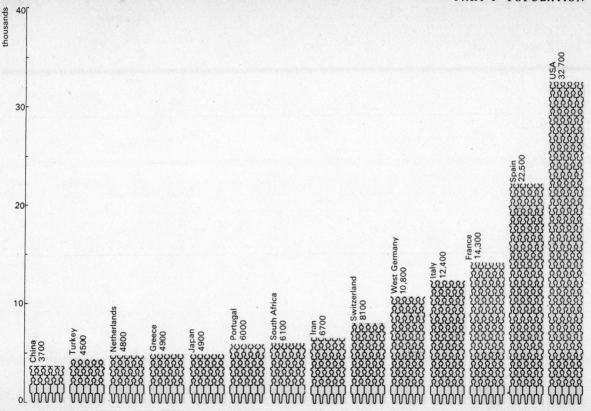

thousands

China 3700 · Turkey 4500 · Netherlands 4800 · Greece 4900 · Japan 4900 · Portugal 6000 · South Africa 6100 · Iran 6700 · Switzerland 8100 · West Germany 10,800 · Italy 12,400 · France 14,300 · Spain 22,500 · USA 32 700

43

Part II
Social

Pensions
Housing
Leisure
Crime
Divorce
Religion

Pensions

Number of persons receiving pensions and benefits: United Kingdom

The number of persons receiving benefits under the *main* provisions of the National Insurance Acts is shown here, as well as Family Allowances, which do not come under the National Insurance scheme. The most dramatic change is clearly the rise in the number of people, especially of women, who are now eligible to draw retirement pensions. This is a simple function of changes in life expectation, shown in the diagram on page 31. If more people survive, more are eligible to claim, and the impact upon government spending can be gauged from the graph on page 131.

Other forms of benefit, which apply to too few people to be shown here, are industrial disablement pensions, which now go to over 200,000 persons a year, and guardians' allowances, which are claimed by about 5,000 persons.

Widows' benefit does not include allowances paid during the first thirteen weeks following the husband's death, but there is a relatively small number of such allowances.

The figures for family allowances show the number of *families* to whom the allowances are paid; the total cost of this benefit is now approximately £360 million a year. One further form of benefit, which like family allowances is not payable under the National Insurance scheme, is Supplementary Benefit. It is not possible to provide comparisons with the other benefits from 1950 to the present because of the changes made when the work of the old National Assistance Board was absorbed into the new Department of Health and Social Security. Supplementary Benefit is now claimed by nearly three million people a year.

Source:
Annual Abstract of Statistics

46

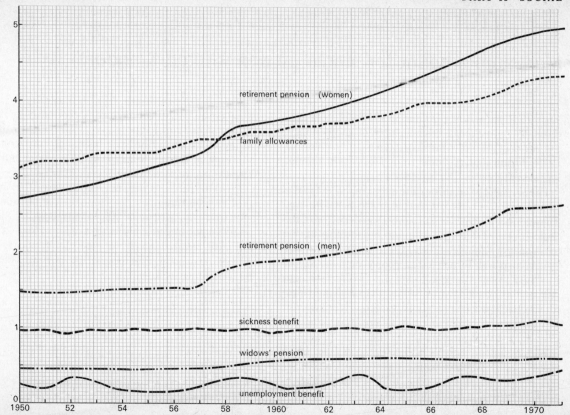

millions

retirement pension (women)

family allowances

retirement pension (men)

sickness benefit

widows' pension

unemployment benefit

1950 52 54 56 58 1960 62 64 66 68 1970

Retirement Pension

Maximum amount for single person: United Kingdom

Since 1909 retirement pensions (often called 'old-age' pensions) have been a basic element in social policy, and opposite we show the maximum sum payable to a single person and the date from which this amount became payable.

Twenty years of argument and agitation, based partly on example from abroad, preceded the first Old Age Pensions Act of 1908. It was closely associated with the name of Lloyd George, who was Chancellor of the Exchequer in Asquith's Liberal government. The weekly five shillings was to be paid to people over the age of 70 whose incomes were not over £21 a year. The sum was seen as a contribution, rather than a living wage. As Churchill put it in a public speech, 'We have not pretended to carry the toiler on to dry land. What we have done is to strap a life-belt around him.'

The metaphor is still appropriate, as the £6·75 payable today probably represents no greater a proportion of 'average earnings' than did the five shillings in 1909. However, a pensioner is eligible nowadays for Supplementary Benefit payments, previously known as National Assistance, but merged with the old Ministry of Pensions and National Insurance into the new Ministry of Social Security in 1966. It is now the Department of Health and Social Security.

The 1909 pensions were non-contributory, but in 1925 they became based on contributions. The pension payable to a married couple has usually been a little less than double the amount for a single person; in 1946 a couple received £2·10, in 1967 £7·30, and in 1972 £10·90. The number of people drawing pensions can be seen on page 47.

Source:
Annual Reports of Ministry of Social Security, and Department of Health and Social Security

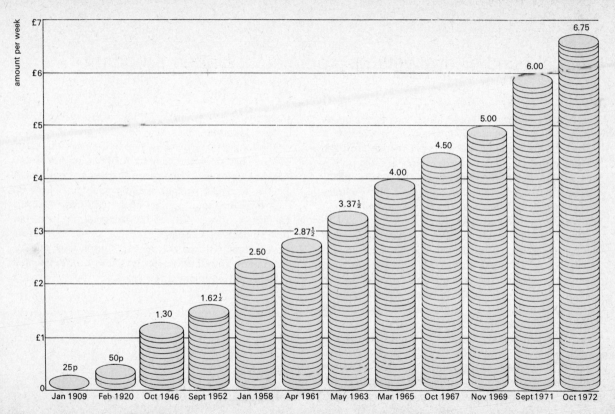

amount per week

£7

£6 — 6.75

£5 — 6.00

£4 — 5.00

£3 — 4.50

£2 — 4.00

£1 — 3.37½

2.87½

2.50

1.62½

1.30

50p

25p

Jan 1909 · Feb 1920 · Oct 1946 · Sept 1952 · Jan 1958 · Apr 1961 · May 1963 · Mar 1965 · Oct 1967 · Nov 1969 · Sept 1971 · Oct 1972

Housebuilding

Annual number of dwellings completed: United Kingdom

The term 'dwellings' refers to all forms of permanent housing, flats, maisonettes and houses. There are a further 10,000 dwellings not included, which are built by public bodies like the armed services and the police. The 'public sector' therefore means the local authorities and the New Towns, and their total also excludes approximately 160,000 temporary houses ('pre-fabs') built between 1945 and 1949.

The pre-war pattern of housing leant heavily towards the private sector. After the war, during which house-building was at a standstill, the pattern was diametrically reversed. The public sector was used as the chosen instrument of housing, with private housing relegated to a minor role. From 1958 the two sectors have been more equal.

The year 1968 marked the peak of house completions, and only in 1967 and 1968 was the target figure of 400,000 dwellings a year reached and passed. Since 1968 the number of completions has fallen, and the number started also fell, which meant that fewer were completed in 1971 and 1972. During these two years, however, housing starts were on a rising trend.

The long-term growth in population has obviously had an effect upon the demand for housing, but so too has the rate of *household formation*, i.e. the number of couples or single persons wishing to set up home on their own. The total number of dwellings exceeded the number of households for the first time in 1966, but any estimates of a 'housing surplus' in the near future must reckon with the two million slum houses due for demolition, as well as old houses likely to be designated as slums during the next few years.

Sources:
Housing Statistics
Annual Abstract of Statistics

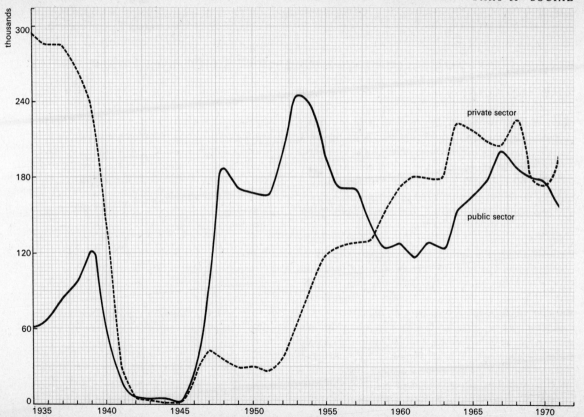

thousands

300

240

private sector

180

public sector

120

60

0

1935   1940   1945   1950   1955   1960   1965   1970

Housebuilding

Number of dwellings completed per 1,000 population: International

If the annual number of dwellings built in a country is divided by the total population (in thousands), the result is a *rate* of housebuilding, which can be compared to the rate for other countries. The United Nations collects and publishes these figures, and the rates for selected countries are compared opposite.

'Dwellings' means houses and flats, built either privately or by public authorities.

Inevitably, the housebuilding programmes of many countries (especially the USSR and Germany) have been dominated by the need to replace housing destroyed by the war, but rising living standards (and expectations), as well as the age of houses built in earlier waves of housebuilding, also have an effect.

A comparison such as this cannot allow for the different standards of what is called 'housing' by the different countries. Where pressure on housing is greatest (for example in Eastern Europe), a new dwelling may be restricted to a small flat of either two or three rooms. In many respects, housing in Britain is the envy of Europe. We have a very high proportion of dwellings equipped with lavatories and baths, and only three European countries have a higher proportion than we do of houses (compared to flats), relative to population. So far as *space standards* are concerned (measured in terms of the number of rooms per 1,000 inhabitants) the British people are probably the best-housed in Europe.

Source:
UN: Annual Bulletin of Housing and Building Statistics for Europe

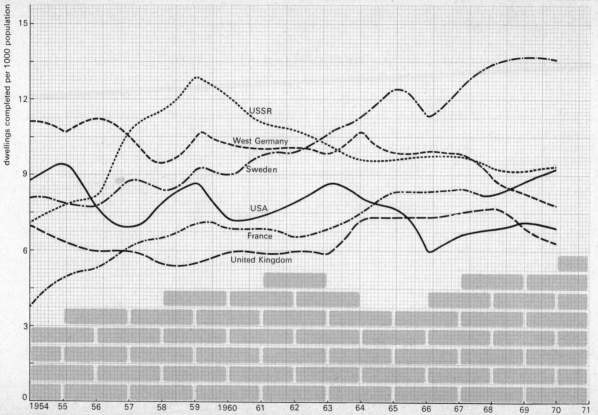

dwellings completed per 1000 population

15

12

USSR

West Germany

Sweden

9

USA

France

6

United Kingdom

3

0

1954 55 56 57 58 59 1960 61 62 63 64 65 66 67 68 69 70 71

Housing

House tenure by income group: United Kingdom

This diagram shows how different types of house tenure (ownership, renting, etc.) vary according to income. The figures are taken from calculations based upon information contained in the 1971 Family Expenditure Survey. The only category not shown opposite is families who live rent-free, a very small proportion of the total.

Incomes, expressed as gross incomes per year, are for *households*. This means that the total income of the main bread-winner is taken, plus husband or wife, plus any income from children who are earning and who have not yet left home. The resultant figure is well above that for the householder alone.

The detailed figures given in the Family Expenditure Survey show that in terms of gross income, families living in privately rented unfurnished dwellings had lower incomes than those in council accommodation. Next come those who have bought their own housing, and best off were those still buying with the aid of a mortgage. No doubt many of those who have completed the purchase of their own housing are now retired and have lower incomes than when they were paying for their mortgage.

The detailed tables in the Survey also permit a comparison between different regions of the country. Home ownership (including homes being currently bought on a mortgage) is highest in East Anglia, where 56·7% of homes are owned, followed by the South-west (54·5%) and the North-west (53·4%). At the other end of the scale, Scotland (26·0%) and the North (38·9%) are the regions where home ownership is rarest. Overall, the Survey shows that nearly 47% of British homes are now owner-occupied.

Source:
Family Expenditure Survey

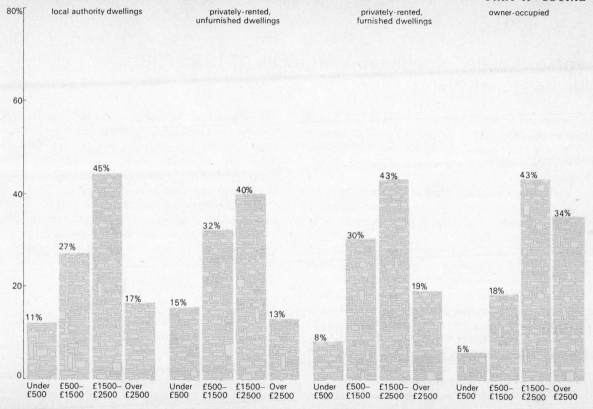

Crime

Persons guilty of indictable offences (1) 1935–68: England and Wales

This series of graphs shows trends in crime in England and Wales, rather than in the United Kingdom, because of the different judicial systems between England and Wales on the one hand and the rest of the UK on the other.

The reader should not draw any exact conclusions from these figures without first reading the cautionary remarks on page 13 concerning the interpretation of the criminal statistics.

The Theft Act of 1968, which came into force on 1 January 1969, redefined theft, and incorporated nearly all offences previously included under larceny, breaking and entering, robbery and embezzlement. The Act also 'increased' the number of indictable offences by including the taking of a motor vehicle without authority, and certain stealing offences.

Thus there is no direct continuity in the pre- and post-1969 statistics, and we have provided separate diagrams for the two separate periods.

The term 'indictable', or 'on the indictment', is a historic phrase in the English legal system which refers, broadly speaking, to the seriousness of the offence. Some offences (e.g. murder) can only be tried on indictment, and must be tried at a Crown Court. Some indictable offences, of lesser gravity, can be tried either in a magistrate's court or in a higher court.

The Criminal Statistics group indictable offences together, and in doing so they grouped (before 1969) a number of specific offences together under certain headings, which are shown in the graph opposite.

Sources:
Criminal Statistics
Annual Abstract of Statistics

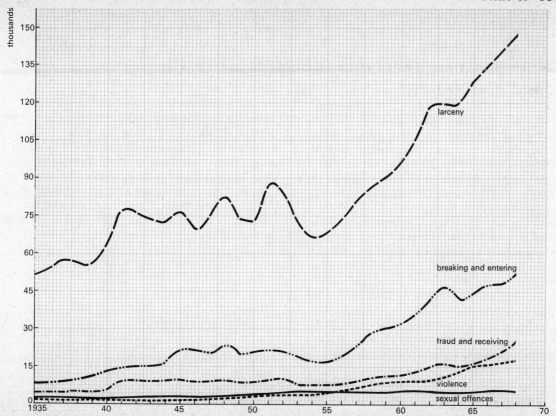

thousands

150

135

120

105

90

75

60

45

30

15

larceny

breaking and entering

fraud and receiving

violence

sexual offences

1935   40   45   50   55   60   65   70

Crime

Persons guilty of indictable offences (2) 1969–71: England and Wales

Here we show the 'new' headings used since the introduction of the Theft Act 1968. These figures should be read in conjunction with those on page 56, but direct comparison with the earlier figures cannot be made, due to the break in continuity. Again, the same caution should be used in interpreting the possible social trends revealed by the figures.

Figures for 'persons found guilty' are not, of course, the same as those for the number of offences known to the police. Not all offences are cleared up, and some people found guilty have committed more than one offence. But the use of 'persons found guilty' does permit a comparison between juvenile and adult offenders (see page 62).

The category of 'violence against the person' consists mainly of wounding (24,700 in 1971). In addition it includes manslaughter (195 in 1971), murder (97) and other offences against the person (250).

The total number of persons found guilty of indictable offences, having risen steadily up to 1970 (323,000 under the new classification), has steadied and shown a slight fall in 1971 (322,000). The decline is due to a reduction in the number of persons found guilty of burglary and theft, which has more than offset the rise in the number found guilty of crimes of violence.

In 1971 the proportion of indictable offences 'cleared up' by the police was 45·4%; this means offences for which a person is arrested or summonsed, or for which he is cautioned.

Sources:
Criminal Statistics
Annual Abstract of Statistics

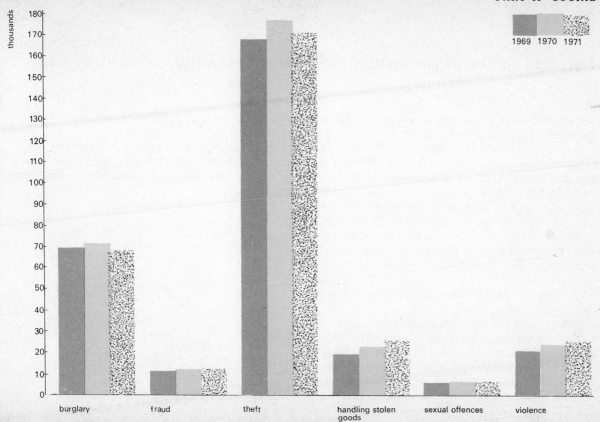

Crime

Persons guilty of non-indictable offences: England and Wales

The offences shown here are the main ones, in terms of the number of persons found guilty.

Mention must be made, however, of one most conspicuous absentee from this graph, and that is persons found guilty of traffic offences. In 1935 there were 400,000 of these, a figure which was reached again and passed in 1956; since then the number has risen to dwarf all other non-indictable offences, and could not be shown to scale on the same graph. In 1971 there were slightly over one million persons found guilty of traffic offences (three quarters of all non-indictable offences).

'Revenue offences' consist mainly of failures to take out licences for dogs and motor cars.

So far as other non-indictable offences are concerned, betting and gaming, once a prominent offence, has shown a much reduced total since the Betting and Gaming Act of 1960 legalized betting shops. Figures are also given in the Criminal Statistics for railway offences, offences against the Education Acts and against the Wireless Telegraphy Acts, and breach of Local Regulations.

Drunkenness includes other offences against the intoxicating liquor laws, but does not include driving while under the influence of drink, which comes under the Highway Acts.

Sources:
Criminal Statistics
Annual Abstract of Statistics

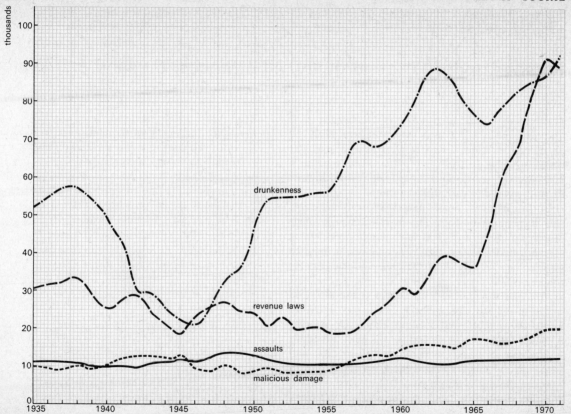

thousands

drunkenness

revenue laws

assaults

malicious damage

1935 1940 1945 1950 1955 1960 1965 1970

61

Juvenile Crime

Persons under 17 found guilty, all offences: England and Wales

The term 'juveniles' as it is employed here means all young persons under the age of 17. This is the age after which a young person can no longer be tried in a juvenile court, sent to an approved school, or dealt with as being in need of care and protection.

Of their offences approximately 60% were indictable and 40% non-indictable. The most prominent single offence in 1971 was theft or unauthorized taking (33,000), followed in turn by offences committed against the Highway Acts (27,000), and burglary or robbery (25,000).

Although the number of juveniles found guilty of offences declined noticeably in 1971 (compared to 1970), the number cautioned by the police rose by a greater proportion. This decline was most noticeable in the case of sexual offences, burglary, theft and handling; the number found guilty of fraud and of violence against the person rose.

In the magistrates' courts the majority of offenders were fined, and most of the remainder received either a conditional discharge or a supervision order.

Overall, juveniles accounted in 1971 for 7% of all persons found guilty of offences, whether indictable or non-indictable. If one omits motoring offences, then they form a higher proportion: 21·4% of indictable offences, and 6·4% of non-indictable.

Sources:
Criminal Statistics
Annual Abstract of Statistics

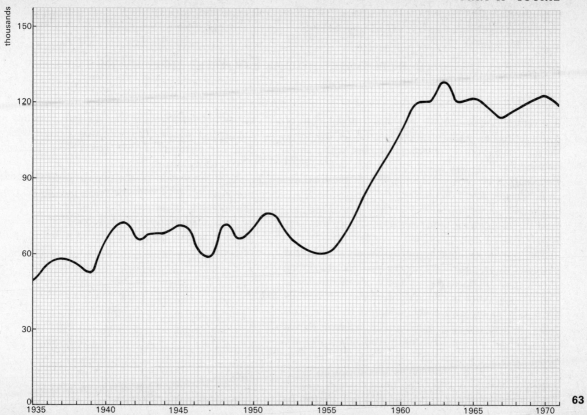

Prisons

Average daily prison population: England and Wales

The graph shows the average daily population of prisons, Borstals and detention centres. Of the total, the great majority are convicted prisoners, with a small number awaiting trial or remanded awaiting medical examination. Approximately one fifth of the total are in Borstals or detention centres.

The overwhelming majority of prisoners at any one time are men, and the total number of women prisoners is only about 1,000.

The rise in the number of prisoners has caused considerable overcrowding in the prisons. According to the latest (1971) Report of the Work of the Prison Department, more than one third of those in custody sleep two or three in a cell designed for one. This overcrowding was not substantially reduced during 1971, but the Prison Department has now embarked upon a large building programme.

The total cost of maintaining the prison service is over £60 million a year. The money comes from a Parliamentary grant, and is offset to a small extent by the £4 million revenue from the sale of goods manufactured in prison. The estimated average weekly net cost per prisoner in 1971 was £23·94 (prisons) and £29·34 (Borstals).

As a proportion of the population, the number of prisoners has risen over the years, but due no doubt to the operation of the probation service and to the system of suspended sentences, the proportion has not risen as fast as the number of persons found guilty of offences.

Sources:
Home Office: Reports of the Work of the Prison Department
Annual Abstract of Statistics

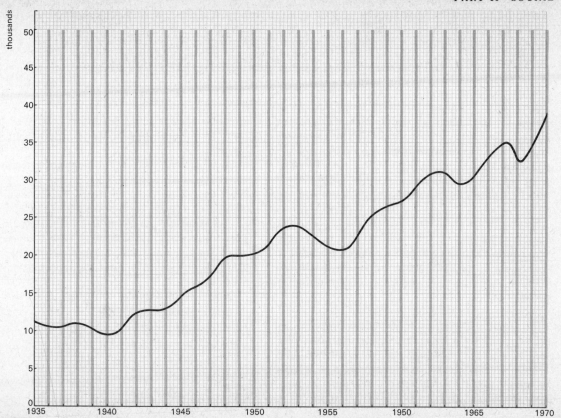

Leisure

Time spent on leisure pursuits: England and Wales

Figures are shown here for the percentage of people's leisure time which they spend on certain activities during weekdays and at weekends.

The data comes from a government report: *Planning for Leisure*, based upon a Government Social Survey study of leisure in urban areas (in which 80% of the population live).

The survey consisted of a sample survey of urban areas, plus separate samples in Inner London and the New Towns. The main aim of the survey was to gather information on people's outdoor physical recreation, as well as excursions and visits to parks and public open spaces.

The main leisure activities are shown here, as well as the variation in the pattern for men and women. In the survey itself a number of other comparisons were used to build up a social profile of leisure pursuits. For example, among young people the main activity was not television but physical recreation (which includes dancing). With marriage, this pattern changes to a predominance of gardening and do-it-yourself (for the men), and crafts and hobbies (mainly knitting) for women.

Social status is another distinguishing feature. The lower the socio-economic class of the respondent, the more television viewing increases. This point may well be related to car ownership; the higher this is, the more time is spent on excursions and visits. *Participation* in physical recreation is also linked with socio-economic class. The higher the class, the greater the participation, although *attendance* at spectator sports is uniform by social class.

Other leisure activities too small to show here are cinema and theatre (1% for men, 1% women), and spectator sports (3% men, 1% women).

Source:
HMSO: *Planning for Leisure*

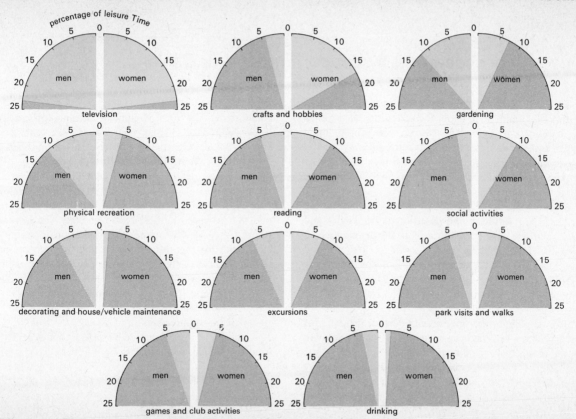

percentage of leisure Time

television

crafts and hobbies

gardening

physical recreation

reading

social activities

decorating and house/vehicle maintenance

excursions

park visits and walks

games and club activities

drinking

Divorce

Divorce proceedings by cause: England and Wales

From 1937 until 1970, under the provisions of the 1937 Matrimonial Causes Act, there were three main 'grounds' for divorce: adultery, desertion and cruelty. Here we show the trends in divorce since that Act by following the pattern of petitions filed under these three main causes.

Where there were petitions based on two or more grounds (e.g. adultery and desertion, or desertion and cruelty), these have been allocated to the heading which was the first of these grounds. Of course, not all petitions for divorce are granted, but the figure for petitions shows the effective 'demand' for divorce. About 90% of petitions are successful, and about two thirds of petitions are filed by wives.

The apparent rise in 'cruelty' as a ground for divorce does not necessarily imply an actual growth in the number of cases of marital cruelty. Increasingly, petitions for divorce in recent years which have been in effect for divorce 'by consent' were obliged to offer apparent causes for marital breakdown which come under the present judicial heading of cruelty.

The figures for 1938 are markedly higher than those for 1937 and before, and this rise in the number of divorces has always been a feature of wartime or of a period following laws which make divorce easier. It represents a 'pent-up' demand which existing legislation had not recognized, and has been a clear feature of the period following the most recent change. The Divorce Reform Act of 1969 came into operation in January 1971, allowing separation as a ground for divorce, and so to the figures shown opposite for 1971 should be added the following *provisional* totals:

Separation (2 years and consent)	16,000
Separation (5 years)	29,900
Separation (consent and 5 years)	5,500

The number of petitions filed in 1971 thus reached a total of 110,000, compared to 70,500 in 1970.

Source:
Annual Abstract of Statistics

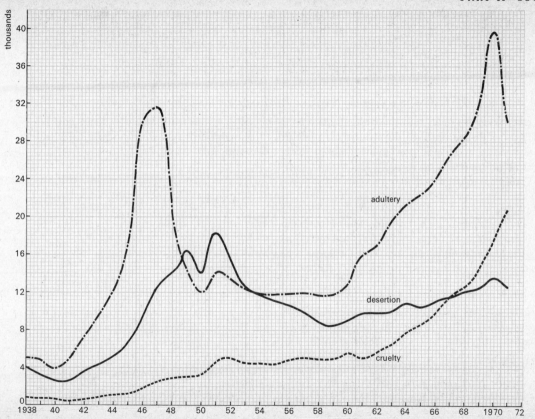

thousands

adultery

desertion

cruelty

1938 40 42 44 46 48 50 52 54 56 58 60 62 64 66 68 1970 72

Divorce

Rate per 1,000 population: International

Inevitably, countries differ in their definitions of divorce, as well as in the accuracy of their statistics, so these comparisons cannot give an exact guide to the 'divorce-proneness' of different countries. In any case, changes in the law can lead to dramatic changes in the statistics from one year to the next.

The figures are the number of divorce decrees granted under civil law, expressed as a proportion of the population (per thousand). Legal separations, and marriages which have been annulled, are not included. The statistics are for 1970, and in a few cases for earlier years.

At the time of writing no figures can be included for countries like Spain or Ireland, because no full legal provision for divorce exists in these countries.

A comparison with the figures published in the first edition of this book shows that the biggest change in recent years has been the rise in the US divorce rate, which was in any case high by comparison with other countries. But the United Nations Demographic Year-book (from which these statistics are drawn) stresses that the 1970 figures for both the USA and USSR must be regarded as provisional.

Source:
United Nations Demographic Yearbook

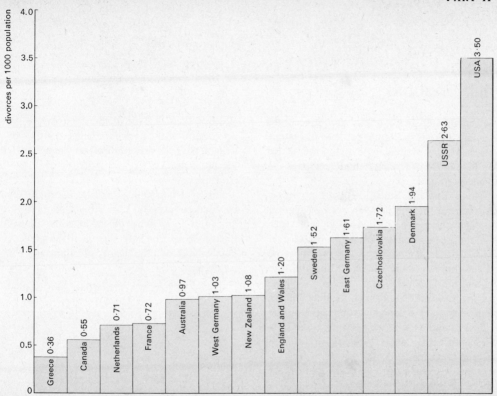

divorces per 1000 population

Greece 0·36
Canada 0·55
Netherlands 0·71
France 0·72
Australia 0·97
West Germany 1·03
New Zealand 1·08
England and Wales 1·20
Sweden 1·52
East Germany 1·61
Czechoslovakia 1·72
Denmark 1·94
USSR 2·63
USA 3·50

Church of England

Membership rates per 1,000 population, at ten-year intervals: England

Church membership statistics, while no doubt accurate in themselves, are a very inadequate guide to the extent of religious activity at a particular time, and the reader should bear in mind the remarks made on page 13 about their interpretation.

The Church of England Statistical Unit publishes detailed statistics for the various degrees of church membership, and these are calculated as rates (per thousand) of the population of the appropriate age. The figures cover the population of the provinces of York and Canterbury, i.e. the whole of England, the Isle of Man, and the Channel Islands.

Confirmation: the total confirmed membership of the Church is shown as a rate per thousand of the population aged 13 and over, as very few boys and girls are confirmed before they are 13. Nearly ten million people have been confirmed.

Baptism: infant baptisms are expressed as the rate per thousand of all live births in a given year.

Electoral Rolls: membership of the church parochial electoral rolls is given as the rate (per thousand) of the population of the appropriate age. Until 1957 membership of the rolls was confined to people over the age of 18, but from 1957 onwards it was available to people from the age of 17.

Easter Communicants: the Church distinguishes between people who take Holy Communion on Easter day, and those who do so at some time during the Easter week. The rate shown in the graph is that for Easter week communicants per thousand of the population aged over 15.

Sources:
Church Information Office: Facts and Figures about the Church of England No. 3
Church of England Year Book

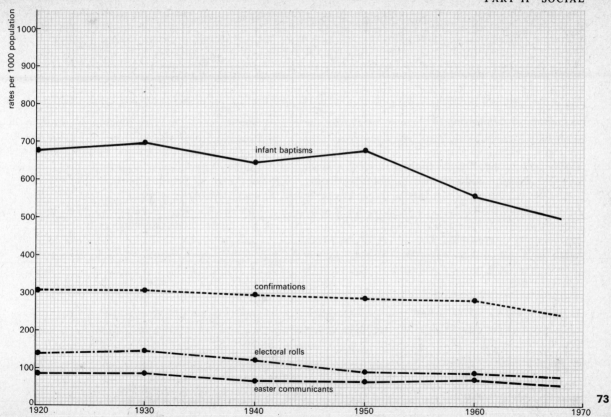

Other Churches

Membership, at ten-year intervals: Great Britain/United Kingdom

Definitions of membership of churches other than the Church of England vary from one denomination to another. The obvious absentee from this membership comparison is the Roman Catholic Church, which publishes figures for the Roman Catholic population as a whole, regardless of church attendance or any other signs of active membership. Thus figures for Roman Catholic membership have been omitted, as they would not be strictly comparable. The total Catholic population of Great Britain, according to the Catholic Directory of 1970, was 3·4 million in 1940, and 4·8 million in 1969.

Similarly, the estimated total of Jews has risen from 160,000 in 1900, to 385,000 in 1940 and 450,000 in 1971.

Baptist Church: figures are for members in the British Isles.

Congregational Church: figures are for members in the United Kingdom. There are no figures for 1920.

Methodist Church: members and probationers in Great Britain and Ireland are included; the number of members in Southern Ireland is relatively few. The figures from 1900 to 1930 are for the Wesleyan Methodist Church, and from 1930 onwards for the Methodist Church as it was constituted (from 1932) after the union between the Primitive, Wesleyan and United Methodist churches.

Church of Scotland: figures are for the total number of communicants on the church rolls.

Sources:

Baptist Handbook
Congregational Year Book
Minutes of Methodist Conference
Church of Scotland Year Book

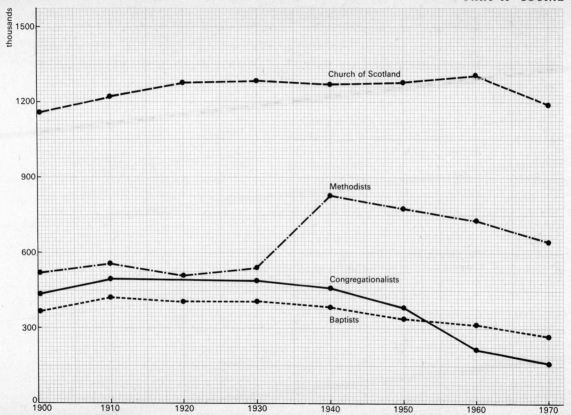

thousands

Church of Scotland

Methodists

Congregationalists

Baptists

1500

1200

900

600

300

0

1900 1910 1920 1930 1940 1950 1960 1970

75

Marriages

Manner of solemnization per 1,000 marriages, at ten-year intervals: England and Wales

Lord Hardwicke's Marriage Act of 1753, which had decreed that no one could be legally married except by a Church of England parson, was repealed in 1836. The Marriage Act which took its place permitted Roman Catholics and Dissenters to be married in their own places of worship, brought into existence Registrars of Births, Marriages and Deaths, and permitted civil weddings.

Since then, as our graph for the period from 1874 onwards shows, the proportion *per thousand marriages* of Church of England weddings has declined, the Roman Catholic proportion has grown, civil ceremonies have increased, and the proportion carried out by other denominations (including Jewish) has declined.

Sources:
Church Information Office: Facts and Figures about the Church of England No. 3
Registrar General's Statistical Review

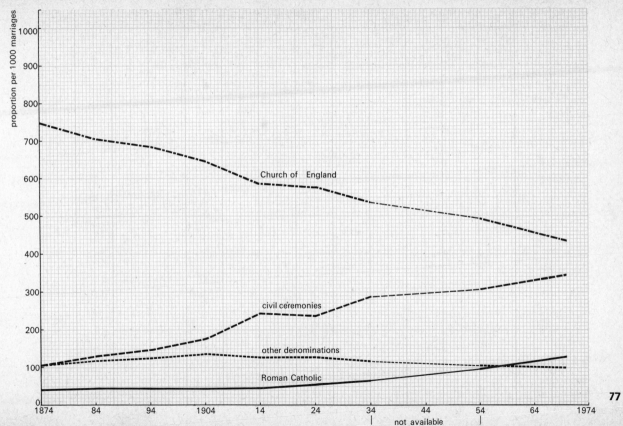

proportion per 1000 marriages

Church of England

civil ceremonies

other denominations

Roman Catholic

1874   84   94   1904   14   24   34   44   54   64   1974

not available

77

Part III
Education

Pupils
Teachers
GCE results
Students
Degrees
Expenditure

Pupils

Number of pupils, by type of school: England and Wales

Because of differences between the educational systems of Scotland, Northern Ireland, and England and Wales, it is not possible to give figures for the whole of the United Kingdom. This graph, and many of the ones which follow, give data for England and Wales. The starting-date, 1947, was the first post-war year in which full statistics were published following the changes made after the 1944 Education Act.

The figures show the total number of pupils in the main types of school in the 'maintained' (i.e. state) system, so the direct-grant grammar schools are not included. There are nearly 200 of these schools, and they contain a further 120,000 pupils.

The only significant omission is the technical school. There were over 300 technical schools in existence after the 1944 Act, but their numbers have dwindled to about 80, and as a distinctive type of school they will no doubt vanish during the period of secondary re-organization.

All children must attend school, so the number of pupils is inevitably a reflection of changing birth-rates. The post-war 'bulge' can be seen passing through the primary schools, and then entering and in turn passing through the secondary schools. This in turn has given way to an even larger bulge, the children of the higher birth-rates of the mid-1950s to mid-1960s.

The decline in the number of modern and grammar school children is of course a direct result of the growth of the numbers in comprehensive schools.

Sources:
Annual Reports of Ministry of Education (1947–53)*
Statistics of Education

* Since the Ministry of Education became the Department of Education and Science statistics have been published under the title: Statistics of Education.

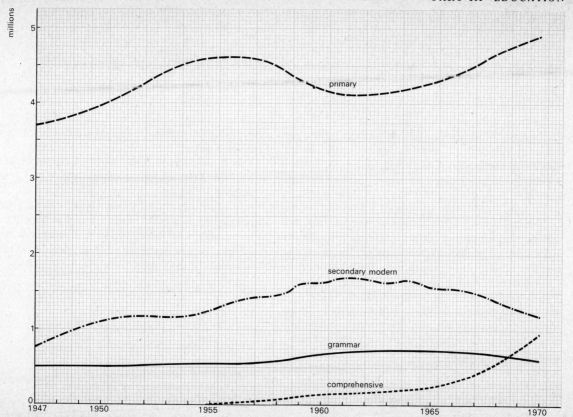

millions

primary

secondary modern

grammar

comprehensive

Teachers

Number of teachers, by type of school: England and Wales

The number of teachers in schools broadly reflects, as would be expected, the changes already shown in the number of pupils. Again, the swing to comprehensives is gradually reducing the totals in grammar and modern schools.

'Schools' here means maintained schools, i.e. those within the state system. Grammar schools do not include the direct-grant grammar schools, which have a further total of about 7,000 teachers. The totals for teachers include full-time teachers, *and* the full-time equivalent of part-time teachers.

In primary schools almost three quarters of the staff are women, whereas in the secondary schools about 60% of the teachers are men. The overall proportion of graduates in the schools is 20%, but this varies by type of school; about 75% of grammar-school staff are graduates, compared with 40% in comprehensives and 16% in secondary modern schools (1970 figures). The great majority of teachers (nearly 90%) have had professional training, either as trained teachers or by doing a postgraduate certificate in education.

With a relatively high 'wastage' rate of about 10% who leave the schools each year, the school system is coming increasingly to rely upon re-entrants to the profession, who now number about 10,000 a year.

Pupil–teacher ratios: there are 27·4 pupils per teacher in primary schools (1970), 18·8 in secondary modern schools, 16·4 in grammar schools, and 17·6 in comprehensives.

Sources:
Annual Reports of Ministry of Education (1947–60)
Statistics of Education

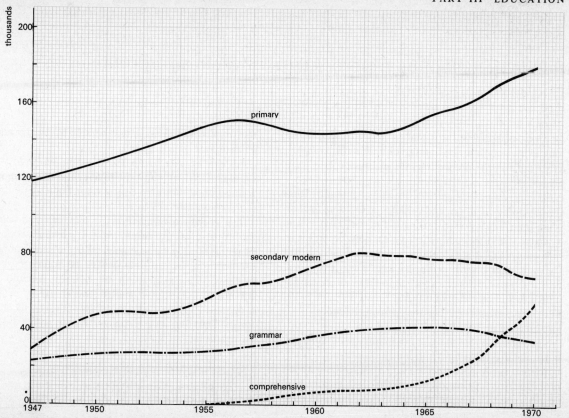

Pupils

Pupils in school as a percentage of their age-group: England and Wales

One way of showing the extent of 'early-leaving' is to look at its opposite, the number of children staying on at school and the proportions these form of their age-group.

Staying on at school has become gradually but steadily more common, and is likely to increase further when the effect is felt of raising the school-leaving age to sixteen, and as comprehensive schools become the rule, rather than the exception, in secondary education. Forward predictions made by the Department of Education and Science expect that 6·9% of eighteen-year-olds will be staying on in 1975, and 8·9% in 1985. These are predictions for the United Kingdom, not just England and Wales.

The figures opposite refer to pupils in *all* schools, maintained, direct-grant, and independent.

The sharp rise between 1963 and 1964 in the number of fifteen-year-olds staying on at school is explained by the provision of the 1962 Education Act which decreed that pupils should no longer be able to leave school at Christmas.

As can be seen from the diagram on page 95, of those children who *do* stay on at school the proportion who go on to full-time education is higher among girls than among boys.

The growth of sixth forms is often seen as being at the expense of 'A' levels, with a growing proportion of pupils staying on to eighteen but not attempting the examination. In fact, this view is not supported by the evidence. The proportion of eighteen-year-old boys leaving school who attempted one or more 'A' levels is around 95%; for girls the proportion is only slightly lower. Thus very few second-year sixth formers do not have a try at 'A' level.

Sources:
Annual Reports of Ministry of Education (1950–59)
Statistics of Education

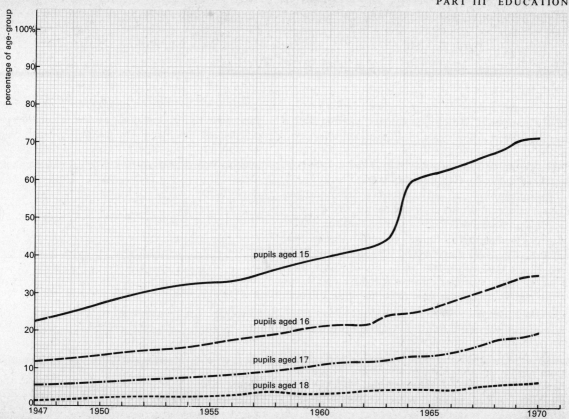

percentage of age-group

pupils aged 15

pupils aged 16

pupils aged 17

pupils aged 18

GCE 'O' Level

Number of passes: England and Wales

In the summer of 1951 pupils sat, for the first time, the new General Certificate of Education, which replaced the old School Certificate. Since then there has been, as can be seen, a steady rise in the number of passes gained in the GCE ordinary level.

The figures show the total number of passes gained in the summer examination each year. Until 1962 the rise was steady, and in 1963 there was an acceleration which was partly due to the 'bulge' in birth-rates in the immediate post-war years; a child born in 1946 or 1947 could have been taking 'O' levels in 1963. Since that time the rise has levelled out, but it must be borne in mind that many schools now offer the alternative of CSE. In a few years' time the pattern of CSE results will become sufficiently clear to enable comparisons to be made with GCE ordinary level.

The pass rate in 1951 was 57·8%, and this figure has risen slightly to around 60%. The pass rate is not, however, a measure of improvement or decline in standards, as there is an element of 'normalization' built into the examination, i.e. an assumption that whether or not standards change a roughly similar proportion of pupils should pass the examination in each successive year.

Source:
Statistics of Education

thousands

boys

girls

750

600

450

300

150

0
1951 52   54   56   58   1960   62   64   66   68   70

87

Passes in different subjects: England and Wales

Given that the number of passes at the GCE ordinary level has increased, it is interesting to see the breakdown of these passes by each individual subject. The number of passes in the different subjects is shown here for the main summer examination in 1971 conducted by the eight examining boards. The totals are provisional Department of Education and Science figures, and are rounded down to the nearest hundred. The subjects shown are the main ones for which candidates entered, and exclude some subjects for which the entry was very small. 'Other arts subjects' include music, craft, and languages other than Latin, French or German.

English language and mathematics are the most popular subjects, and are necessary both for pupils who want to stay on to the sixth form and for those who intend to leave for employment.

A look at the pattern of different subjects over the decade since 1961 shows some clear changes in the relative 'importance' of these subjects. The most massive rise (up by 290%) is in Economics, followed at a distance by 'other social science subjects' (increased by 91%). Science subjects such as Biology (87% up) and Physics (59%) are next, and at the bottom of the list are History (only 7% up) and Latin, for which there has actually been a drop in enrolment and a decline in the overall number of passes by 3%.

Source:
Statistics of Education

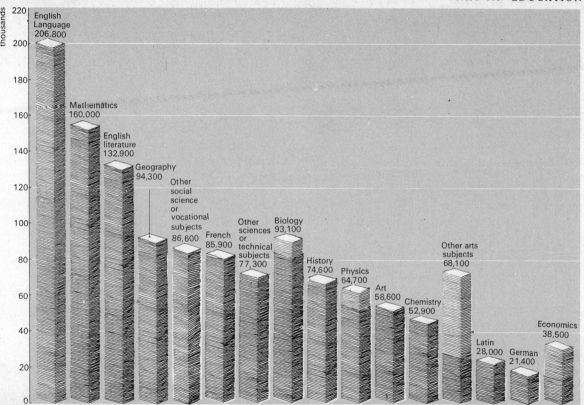

thousands

English Language 206,800
Mathematics 160,000
English literature 132,900
Geography 94,300
Other social science or vocational subjects 86,600
French 85,900
Other sciences or technical subjects 77,300
Biology 93,100
History 74,600
Physics 64,700
Art 58,600
Chemistry 52,900
Other arts subjects 68,100
Latin 28,000
German 21,400
Economics 38,500

GCE 'A' Level

Number of passes: England and Wales

In this graph, the 'bulge' generation can be seen to have moved on from 'O' levels and into the sixth forms, where it swelled the total of 'A'-level passes in 1965. But the growth in 'A'-level passes due to the bulge was superimposed on what was in any case a clear upward trend. This growth has taken place partly in the technical colleges, as well as the schools, but still only 10% of 'A' levels are taken in the colleges.

If we look, not just at the total of 'A' levels, but at the proportion of pupils who get *two or more* 'A' levels (the minimum university entrance requirement), we find that this proportion has exceeded the predictions of the Robbins Committee, and now represents around 11% of the age-group.

These changes have had important implications for university entrance. The Robbins Committee recommended that the universities should provide places for 65% of those who obtained two or more 'A' levels. Of course, this does not mean that the universities should only meet 65% of the 'demand' for places. Not all successful school-leavers wish to go to university, and many who wish to go do not have high enough grades to satisfy the actual entrance requirements laid down by the various universities. It seems that the universities meet about 80% of the *effective* demand in a given year. But the recommended 65% has in fact fallen to about 58%, and has meant keener competition for university places in some subjects. Acceptance rates range from about 80% of applicants in pure science subjects, to about 50% in social science.

Sources:
Annual Reports of Ministry of Education
Statistics of Education

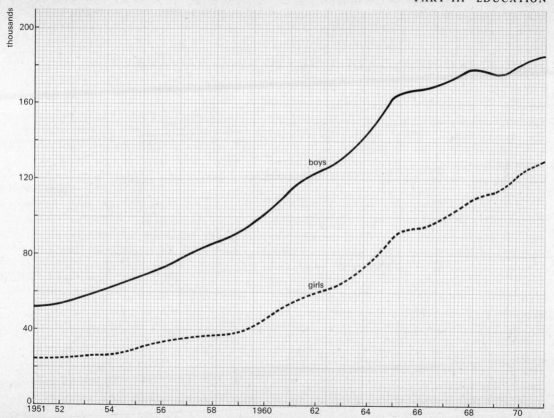

thousands

200

160

120

80

40

0

boys

girls

1951 52   54   56   58   1960   62   64   66   68   70

GCE 'A' Level

Passes in different subjects: England and Wales

We complete the picture of GCE results by giving the number of passes in different subjects at advanced level – also for the summer examination of 1971. The totals are provisional Department of Education and Science figures, and are rounded down to the nearest hundred.

Mathematics heads the field, closely followed by English literature. Both of these are 'key' subjects, in that they may be required as a basic ingredient of pairs or trios of subjects needed for university entrance.

Although Mathematics has the highest number of passes, with Physics not far behind, it is the arts and social science subjects (especially Economics) which have grown at 'A' level in recent years, following a period in the 1950s when the growth area was the natural sciences. This 'swing to the arts' has affected the pattern of subjects studied at university. The large total for Economics includes that for Economic History and British Constitution.

The percentage of passes in 1951 was 73%; this has dropped now to around 68%, but as in the case of 'O' levels the examination system deliberately passes a fairly consistent percentage of candidates from year to year.

As with the 'O' level results, one can make a comparison between the relative prominence of different subjects over the past ten years. As we have noted, easily the largest growth area has been the 'other social science and vocational subjects' (up by 493%), but part of this rise is due to the expansion in teaching of General Studies, which was originally introduced in 1959. Economics has boomed (up by 284%), as has Biology (216%), and at the other end of the scale there has been a decline in the number of passes in Botany and Zoology (down by 56% and 39%) and again in Latin, which declined by 25%.

Source:
Statistics of Education

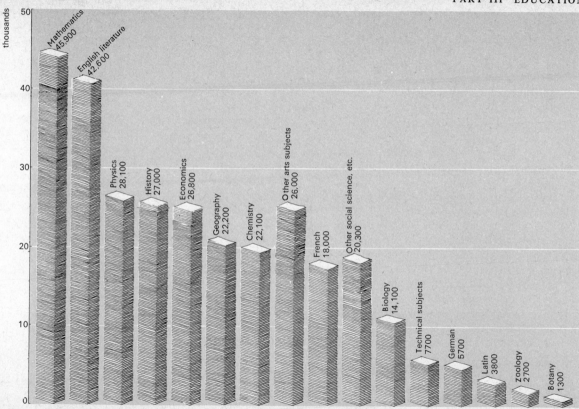

thousands

Mathematics
45,900

English literature
42,600

Physics
28,100

History
27,000

Economics
26,800

Geography
22,200

Chemistry
22,100

Other arts subjects
26,000

French
18,000

Other social science, etc.
20,300

Biology
14,100

Technical subjects
7700

German
5700

Latin
3800

Zoology
2700

Botany
1300

School Leavers

Percentage going on to full-time further and higher education: England and Wales

Different types of secondary schools send different proportions of their school-leavers on to full-time further and higher education, ranging from 7·7% of boys in secondary modern schools to 68·1% of girls in direct-grant schools. The remainder of the pupils go directly into employment, with or without part-time study. The figures are for the school year 1969–70.

'Other' secondary schools include technical schools, multilateral and bilateral schools. The heading 'Independent schools' refers to those schools which are recognized as efficient by the Department of Education and Science. Not all academically-minded independent schools seek recognition, but most do, so this heading is likely to include the academically strongest independent schools and does not refer to the whole range of schools outside the state system.

The figure for 'all schools' thus also excludes independent schools not recognized as efficient, as well as special schools.

The higher percentage of girls who go on to further studies is accounted for partly by the higher proportion who go on to colleges of education (approximately 5·0% of girls in all schools, as opposed to 1·5% of boys), as well as those who go on to other forms of further education (including secretarial training). So far as *higher* education is concerned (mainly the universities, polytechnics, and degree courses in colleges of technology) the boys outnumber the girls. The percentage of boys going on to higher education is approximately 9%, as compared to 5% for girls.

Source:
Statistics of Education

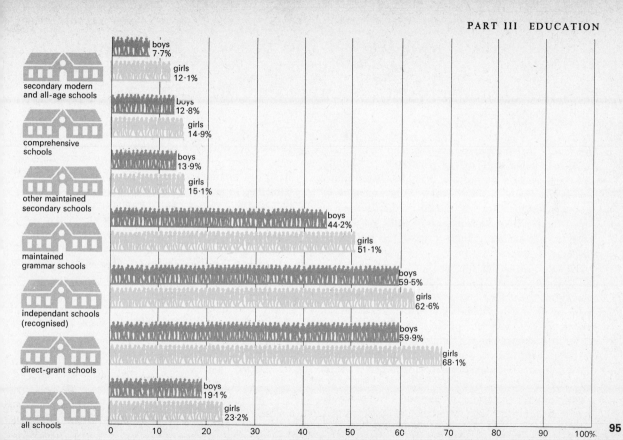

secondary modern
and all-age schools

boys
7·7%

girls
12·1%

comprehensive
schools

boys
12·8%

girls
14·9%

other maintained
secondary schools

boys
13·9%

girls
15·1%

maintained
grammar schools

boys
44·2%

girls
51·1%

independant schools
(recognised)

boys
59·5%

girls
62·6%

direct-grant schools

boys
59·9%

girls
68·1%

all schools

boys
19·1%

girls
23·2%

0   10   20   30   40   50   60   70   80   90   100%

Teacher Training

Number of students completing teacher training: United Kingdom

The rise in the number of students who successfully complete teacher training is remarkable. A fairly stationary position during the 1950s has been transformed into one of rapid growth, with the exception of the dip in numbers in 1962 caused by the decision to extend the basic course from two to three years. This expanded the colleges, but restricted the output of teachers that year.

The totals given here include colleges of education and university departments of education, so there are now about 8,000 men and women included who are doing one-year postgraduate certificates in education. The figures are for the end of the summer term in each of the years shown, and the totals exclude the approximately 36,000 men and women trained under the one-year Emergency Training Scheme which operated from 1945 to 1951.

The rise in the birth-rate from the mid-1950s onwards, combined with the high 'wastage' rate of women teachers, led to a crisis of teacher supply in the early 1960s. The colleges of education were requested to provide a total of 80,000 places by 1970–71, and the Robbins Committee on Higher Education recommended a further expansion to provide 111,000 places in the colleges by 1973–4. On current trends, both these recommended figures will be comfortably passed, and this has proved possible without any significant decline in entry standards, so far as these can be gauged from 'O'-and 'A'-level qualifications. Over 60% of entrants have one or more 'A' levels.

Sources:
Statistics of Education
Scottish Educational Statistics
N. Ireland: Reports of Ministry of Education

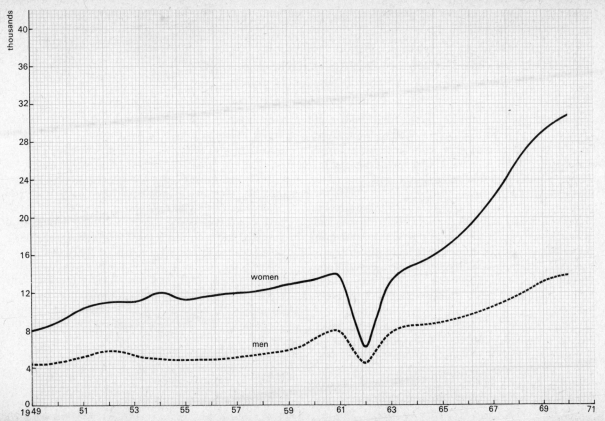

Students

Number of full-time students: United Kingdom

This graph shows both the rise in the number of students, and the slight but perceptible slowing down in this rate of increase. The figures are for *full-time* university students studying at undergraduate level on courses leading to a first degree or diploma, as well as those studying as advanced students.

In addition to these totals, there are approximately 3,000 men and 2,000 women *part-time* undergraduate students studying at the same level, and 15,000 men and 3,000 women *part-time* postgraduate students.

From 1945–6 onwards the figures have included the former University Colleges (e.g. Hull, Leicester), and from 1965–6 the former Colleges of Advanced Technology.

The overall rise in the number of places in higher education has had a number of implications. Taken with the growth in teacher training, it represents an increase in the proportion of the appropriate age-group who will be entering higher education, and this is now nearly 15%. It means for some applicants (particularly in the social sciences and humanities) that the competition to obtain places at university has become keener. And it also represents a growth in higher education (that is, students studying for degrees or at equivalent level) *outside* the universities. During the academic year 1970–71 there were approximately 12,500 men and 5,000 women studying full-time for university or CNAA first degrees in Polytechnics and other grant-aided colleges, and a further 13,000 men and 1,000 women doing degrees by sandwich courses in the same colleges.

The total number of students *within* the universities has kept pace with, and now slightly exceeded, the recommendations of the Robbins Committee on Higher Education. So far as all further and higher education is concerned, the numbers comfortably exceed the Robbins projections.

Sources:
Statistics of Education
U.G.C. Returns from Universities

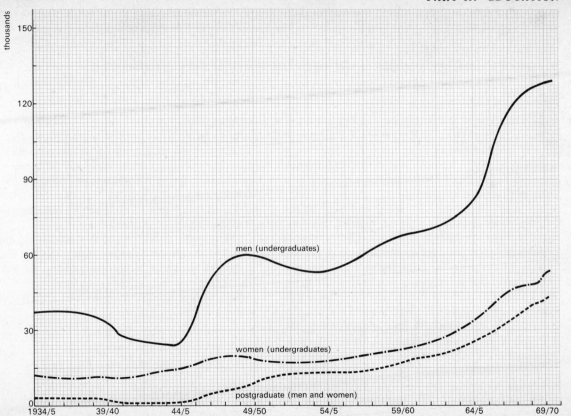

thousands

men (undergraduates)

women (undergraduates)

postgraduate (men and women)

Degrees

First degree subjects studied by university students: United Kingdom

Ideally, it would be possible to show an historical run of figures, comparing the pattern of choices for degree subjects over a period of time. In 1965–6, however, a new system of classification was introduced for the different groups of subjects, and so continuity was lost. There are over 500 separate degree courses and combinations of courses one can take at university, so for statistical purposes they must be grouped under a limited number of broad headings. The headings shown opposite are the 'new' ones employed since 1966.

The figures relate to the academic year 1970–71, and include all *full-time* university students studying at *undergraduate* level.

The headings used may need amplifying a little. Education at undergraduate level means mainly the Bachelor of Education, as some universities include B.Ed. students in their undergraduate returns. Medicine includes dentistry and pharmacy. Engineering and technology includes all forms of engineering, as well as mining, surveying, and metallurgy. Agriculture includes forestry, and veterinary science. Science includes geology, as well as mathematics, chemistry, and physics. Social, administrative and business studies includes psychology, sociology, law, economics and government. Under Architecture and other professional subjects come vocational courses like town planning, and hotel management, and Other Arts includes history, theology, philosophy, drama, art and music.

The 'growth' areas have been social science and the arts, and the universities have largely met the demand caused by the swing to these subjects in the schools. This swing was not welcomed by the Dainton Committee, who urged that it should be reversed in the schools.

Source:
Statistics of Education

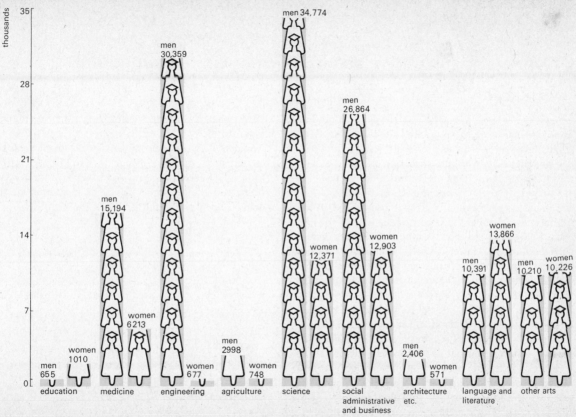

thousands

35

28

21

14

7

0

men 34,774

men
30,359

men
15,194

men
26,864

women
13,866

women
12,903

women
12,371

men
10,391

men
10,210

women
10,226

women
6 213

men
655

women
1010

women
677

men
2998

women
748

men
2,406

women
571

education   medicine   engineering   agriculture   science   social administrative and business   architecture etc.   language and literature   other arts

Degrees

University results, by class of degree: United Kingdom

University degrees, like GCE 'A' levels, are graded. The distribution of these grades, known as 'classes', is illustrated here for finals exams in 1970. All universities are included, with the exception of internal and external degrees of London University when they are awarded to students outside the university sector.

The system of classing degrees is nearly, but by no means entirely, universal. It consists usually of the first class, followed by divisions one and two of the second class ('upper' and 'lower' seconds), followed by a third class, and in many cases followed in turn by a pass or ordinary degree. This last category may be a course for which students register when they enter university, or it may be used as a course to which students are relegated if they fail a qualifying examination.

In a few cases (mainly Oxford and Cambridge), the second class degree is not divided into two divisions, so there is a category opposite of 'undivided second'. 'Other honours' means third class degrees, with the addition of a few fourth class and aegrotats.

In terms of academic performance, the men students seem to be very slightly more successful than the women: 7·7% of men students took firsts, compared to only 4·2% of women students, but 24·2% of women took upper seconds, compared to 22% of men. At the other end of the scale, 22·5% of men took pass or ordinary degrees, as did 22·9% of the women.

Source:
Statistics of Education

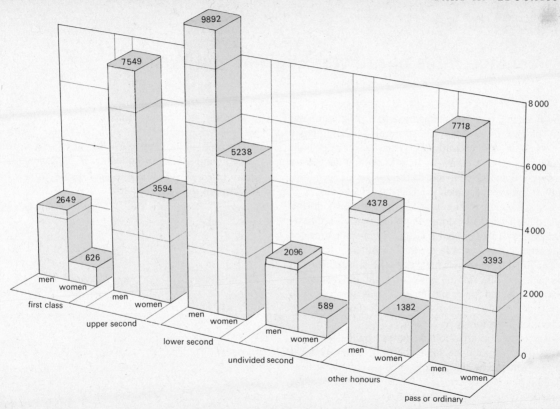

Educational Expenditure

Percentage rates of growth: England and Wales

The financial year 1959–60 is used as a 'base' and the percentage *rates* of growth in spending, in the different branches of the educational system, are calculated between then and 1969–70. It is important to realize that we are not looking here at the *amount* of spending, only at the pace at which it has grown since 1959.

Educational spending as a whole has grown during this period (in real terms, it has grown at approximately five to six per cent a year), but in some areas of education it has grown faster than in others.

The main beneficiaries have been the universities and the colleges. The rate of growth for the universities is partly accounted for by the fact that their numbers were swollen by additions from the ranks of the Colleges of Advanced Technology in 1965–6.

Expenditure in this context means public spending (with the exception of loan charges), both by local authorities and by the government, current as well as capital, but not of course private spending by individuals.

The only public expenditure omitted is what is known as 'related expenditure', such as school meals and milk (£102 million in 1969–70), grants to university students and education students (£60 million combined), and a range of smaller items such as the school health service and the youth service.

Source:
Statistics of Education

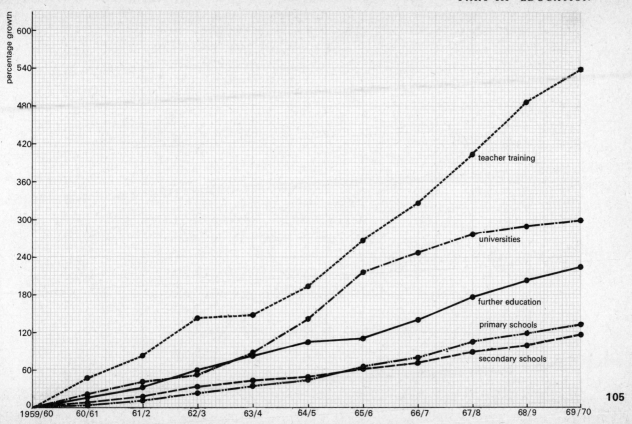

percentage growth

teacher training

universities

further education

primary schools

secondary schools

1959/60 60/61 61/2 62/3 63/4 64/5 65/6 66/7 67/8 68/9 69/70

105

Part IV
Labour

Working hours
Trade Unions
Strikes
Unemployment

Hours Worked

Average weekly hours worked by men over 21: United Kingdom

Here we have a graph in which the 'base' for the vertical axis is forty, rather than zero. This has the effect of showing up variations in working hours which would not be visible on a scale of, say, zero to one hundred.

The hours are the average weekly hours *actually worked* by men aged over twenty-one, who comprise the bulk of the labour force and for whom there is a comparable run of figures since 1938. There is a gap, however, from 1939 to 1942, when no records were available.

The reference to hours actually worked means that the figures include overtime, and do not show the trend in the *negotiated* working week. The striking point about this series is how little the working week has actually shortened since the late 1930s. What has happened is that although the 'basic' or negotiated working week has come down considerably, people have preferred to work as long as before but at overtime rates. Workers in manufacturing industries work in the region of eight hours overtime a week. The figures in the graph are for manufacturing and certain other industries, which include transport and public administration.

These figures help to put arguments about the 'problem of leisure' into perspective. If one compares the present day with the late nineteenth century we no doubt have much more leisure time, including the likelihood of a five- instead of a six-day week. But if we compare with the 1930s, there has been little change.

From 1943 to 1945 the figures are for July of each year, from 1946 to 1948 and 1960 to 1970 for October, and in the remaining years for April.

Sources:
Department of Employment Gazette
Annual Abstract of Statistics

hours worked per week

not available

Hours Worked

Average weekly hours in manufacturing industries: International

It is important to note that the range of figures on the horizontal axis of the diagram is a narrow one, and that it starts at a base of thirty instead of zero. This has the (intended) effect of 'exaggerating' the differences between the figures for different countries.

Britain stands neither high nor low in a league table of working hours. Unlike the figures given on page 109, these international comparisons are averages which include both men and women. In most countries women work a shorter working week, and their inclusion brings down the average figure. The figures are for 1970.

The hours are hours *actually worked* in the manufacturing industries of the various countries, with the exception of the USA, West Germany, New Zealand and Switzerland, where the figures are for hours *paid for*. Thus the figures for all countries include overtime and time spent in short rest-periods at the place of work.

In general, hours of work have come down in the industrial countries, although figures are rarely collected for hours of work in jobs outside manufacturing. Working hours in industries like agriculture are, in any case, almost impossible to define.

One point to note is that in Britain the number of days worked in the whole year is higher than that for most of the countries shown here. In the United Kingdom, in 1970, two out of every five manual workers still only had two weeks paid holiday a year. In France there is a state-guaranteed minimum of four weeks annual holiday, and both France and other European countries take more days off per year for religious holidays and for local equivalents of our bank holidays.

Source:
ILO Yearbook of Labour Statistics

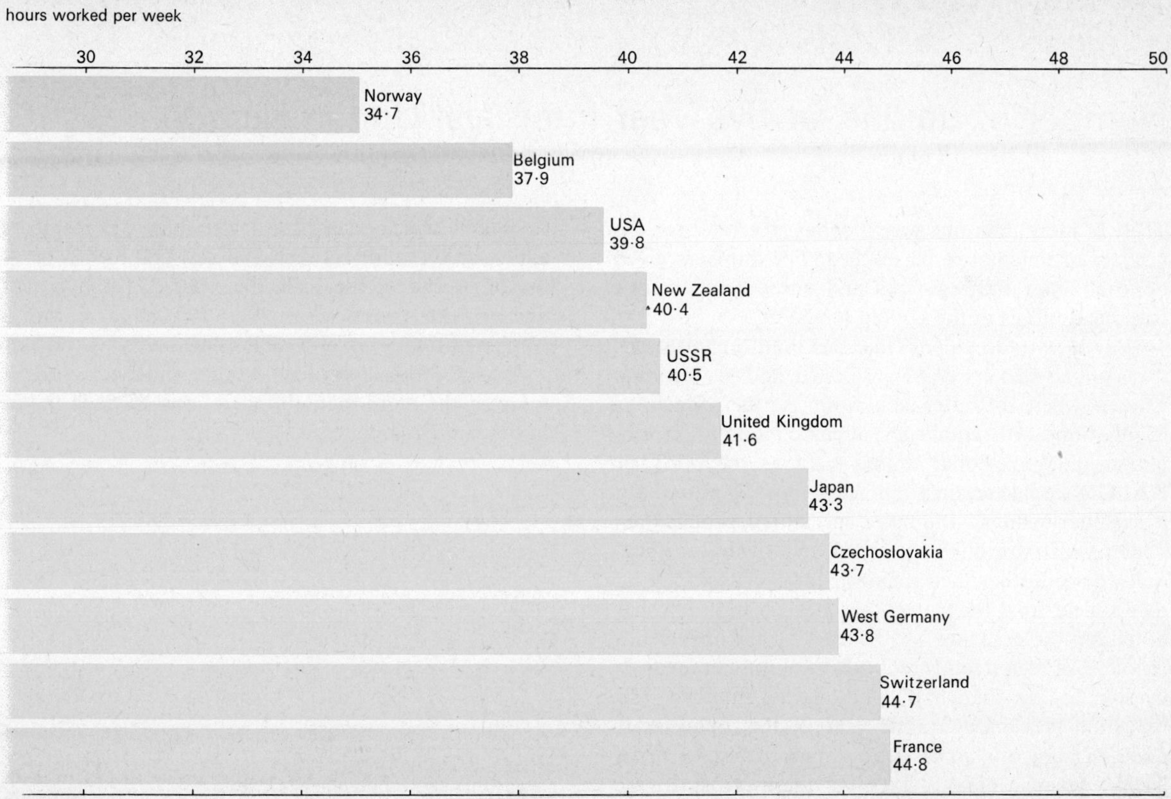

hours worked per week

30	32	34	36	38	40	42	44	46	48	50

Norway
34·7

Belgium
37·9

USA
39·8

New Zealand
40·4

USSR
40·5

United Kingdom
41·6

Japan
43·3

Czechoslovakia
43·7

West Germany
43·8

Switzerland
44·7

France
44·8

Trade Unions

Number of unions, at five-year intervals: United Kingdom

There is more than one way in which the total for the number of unions can be reached. The numbers given opposite show the registered and unregistered unions with head offices in the United Kingdom.

The term 'trade unions' includes both organizations for manual workers *and* for salaried and professional workers where the latter include among their functions negotiations with employers about conditions of employment. White-collar unions such as the NUT or NALGO would certainly fall within this definition, but it excludes some of the more specialized professional bodies which are only concerned to provide qualifications, or to further their members' knowledge.

It is clear from the figures that the very large number of unions in existence at the end of the nineteenth century has been steadily reduced, by closure or amalgamation, to less than half their original number. The reduction has been mainly among the small craft unions, many of which have amalgamated to form larger 'general' unions. Even so, there are still over 90 unions which each have fewer than 100 members, and over 100 with between 100 and 500 members. At the other end of the scale there are 23 large general unions with membership over 100,000 and with a combined total of over 7 million members.

A large proportion of unions are affiliated to one or more of the more than 40 federations of trade unions in the United Kingdom.

Sources:
Abstracts of Labour Statistics
Annual Abstract of Statistics
Department of Employment Gazette

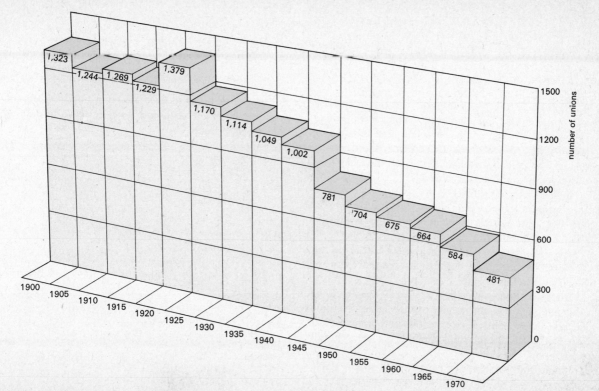

number of unions

1,323
1,244
1,269
1,229
1,379
1,170
1,114
1,049
1,002
781
704
675
664
584
481

1900 1905 1910 1915 1920 1925 1930 1935 1940 1945 1950 1955 1960 1965 1970

1500
1200
900
600
300
0

Trade Unions

Number of members, at five-year intervals: United Kingdom

At the end of the nineteenth century one employed man in seven and one employed woman in thirty-five belonged to a trade union. Now one man in two is a member, and one woman in four. Opposite we trace this growth of union membership since the early part of the century, at five-year intervals.

As in the case of the total number of unions, membership includes those organizations with head offices in the UK, and which negotiate for their members, whether white-collar or blue-overall.

Some members may be counted twice if they belong to more than one union, but it is believed that there are few people in this position.

Totals for women members are partly estimated, as some unions are unable to give precise figures. In some areas of the economy, such as textiles and some medical services, female membership outnumbers male membership.

Union membership shows a much more stable pattern nowadays than it did between the wars, but at all times it is liable to fluctuate according to economic conditions. Severe economic restraint tends to depress membership levels.

Sources:
Abstracts of Labour Statistics
Annual Abstract of Statistics

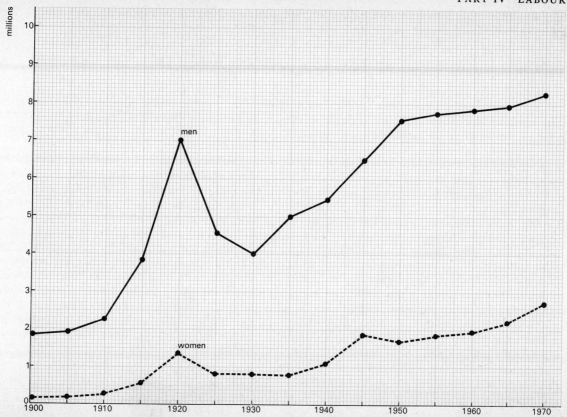

Strikes

Annual number of stoppages: United Kingdom

The simplest and most basic measure of strikes is the total number which begin in any one year, and this changing pattern for strikes in all industries and services is shown opposite. Both official and unofficial strikes are included.

Within the term 'all industries and services', however, are important variations from industry to industry. During the 1930s the number of strikes in the mining industry was much greater than in any other industry. During the war years and during the 1950s and early 1960s mining continued to dominate the annual totals. During the past few years, however, mining has come to take second place to strikes in the metals, engineering, shipbuilding and vehicle industries. In 1971 there were 234 strikes in the construction industry, 138 in mining, 635 in metal manufacturing and engineering, 242 in the motor vehicle industry, 269 in transport and communication, and 97 in the textile and clothing industries combined. There were 613 strikes in other industries. Stoppages which include fewer than ten workers, or which last less than one day, are excluded, unless the total number of working days lost comes to more than one hundred.

The Department of Employment provides a breakdown of stoppages according to their ostensible cause. In 1971, of the total of 2,228 stoppages, 890 were claims for wage and salary increases, 265 were other disputes concerned with wages, 57 were demarcation disputes, 83 concerned the trade union status of employees, 451 were concerned with the employment or sacking of workers, 362 with rules and discipline, and the remainder were a small number connected with hours of work, personnel policy, and sympathetic action. A comparison of these 'causes' of stoppages over the last few years shows that wage claims have become a more and more predominant cause of disputes at work.

Sources:
Department of Employment Gazette
Annual Abstract of Statistics

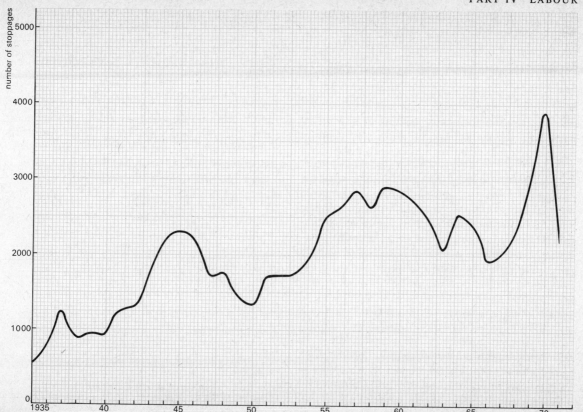

number of stoppages

Strikes

Number of workers involved in stoppages: United Kingdom

As in the case of the annual number of strikes, the figures are for the number of workers involved in official and unofficial strikes and lockouts *beginning* in each year.

The official figures for stoppages include the total number of workers *directly* or *indirectly* involved in the disputes. So it is possible that where some workers have been involved in more than one stoppage they will be counted more than once in the year's total. This also means that workers thrown out of work at the establishments where the disputes occurred are also included in the figures, although they themselves were not involved in the dispute. In 1971 just under 1½ million workers were directly involved in strikes, and only 330,000 were indirectly involved. The very high total of workers involved in 1962 was due to a short but very widespread strike in the engineering industries.

The characteristic pattern of industrial conflict in Britain is for short, sharp action which only lasts for a day or two. In 1971 21% of strikes were for not more than one day, 17% were for over one and not more than two days, and a further 13% lasted for more than two but less than three days. The pattern of duration of strikes was 'stretched' somewhat in 1971 by the prolonged postal dispute.

Sources:
Department of Employment Gazette
Annual Abstract of Statistics

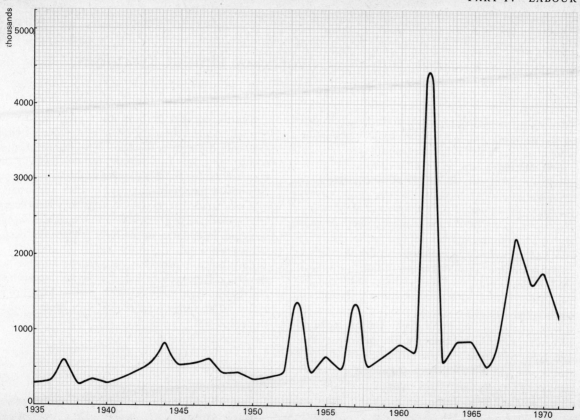

thousands

Strikes

Working days lost, five-year averages: United Kingdom

To complete the picture of industrial disputes provided on the preceding pages, it is necessary to examine the amount of time which is lost through strikes.·

It is difficult to look at the amount of time lost to industry in recent years without the perspective provided by events earlier in the century, so this graph surveys the whole of the period since the turn of the century. The figures are for the average number of working days lost over a five-year period.

A time of widespread industrial conflict during the 1890s gave way to relative quiescence during the early years of this century, but this was dispelled by massive strikes in 1912 and 1919, mainly in mining, textiles and engineering. The 1920s were a period of persistent industrial conflict, culminating in the general strike of 1926, when a total of 162 million working days were lost. The 1950s and 1960s, by contrast, show much lower totals, although it should be borne in mind that the number of days in the average working week has also been reduced in this period.

Figures for working days lost in disputes are not normally able to show the extent of time lost in establishments other than the ones in which the disputes occur. But the Department of Employment has obtained figures about a number of instances of repercussions in the motor industry. In 1971, for instance, it is estimated that 95,000 working days were lost in establishments other than those in which the disputes occurred, in addition to the three million days lost in the industry itself.

To provide a perspective through which time lost through disputes can be judged, it is worth remembering that at least twice as much time is lost through industrial accidents, and around fifty times as much through illness.

Sources:
Department of Employment Gazette
Abstracts of Labour Statistics

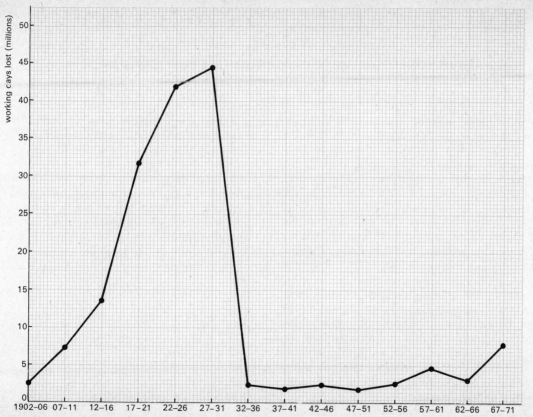

Strikes

Working days lost, ten-year averages: International

The internationally accepted way of comparing the extent of striking in different countries is to take the annual number of days lost through industrial disputes *per thousand workers* in the labour force. These figures are based upon data compiled by the International Labour Office, and are averages for the whole of the ten-year period 1961–70. Thus individual fluctuations from year to year are ironed out, and although the definitions of strikes vary slightly from country to country, the comparisons give a fair picture of industrial conflict on a comparative basis.

The industries covered are mining, construction, manufacturing and transport, and it is within these industries that in most countries (and certainly in Britain) the overwhelming majority of strikes occur. The only exceptions to this classification are the figures for Australia and the USA which include the gas and electricity industries, those for Denmark which are confined to manufacturing, and those for Sweden which cover all industries.

Compared with other industrial countries, Britain has a fairly moderate strike record, at least so far as the amount of time lost is concerned. The United States, with its vigorously competitive economy, always has a high strike record, accompanied by Italy, in which mass strikes covering whole industries are common. At the other end of the scale, and not shown on this diagram, is Switzerland, where an annual average of five working days per thousand workers was lost in this period.

Source:
Department of Employment Gazette

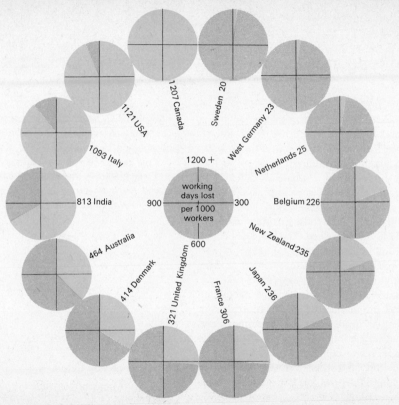

1 207 Canada
1121 USA
1093 Italy
813 India
464 Australia
414 Denmark
321 United Kingdom
France 306
Japan 236
New Zealand 235
Belgium 226
Netherlands 25
West Germany 23
Sweden 20

1200 +
working
days lost
900 per 1000 300
workers
600

Unemployment

Number of registered unemployed persons: United Kingdom

After the high levels of unemployment during the inter-war years, the level inevitably fell during the period of the war, and since then has fluctuated in a cyclic way.

The figures include all unemployed persons on the registers of the Employment Exchanges except for people who are so severely disabled that they are unable to work except under special conditions. From 1935 to 1948 the totals were those for July of each year, and since 1948 they have been the totals for June.

The number of unemployed since 1966–7 has remained unexpectedly high, and represented a little over 3% of the total number of employees in 1971. At first, there seems to have been a demand for labour in the economy, and the number of registered vacancies remained as great as in years of low unemployment like 1964. It was argued that better social security benefits may have been acting as a 'cushion' for a longer period between jobs, or, alternatively, employers may have been cutting down on staff after a long period of labour hoarding. Unemployment of 1970–72, however, has risen and has been a reflection of more deep-seated trends in the economy. It has been accompanied by a very low level of registered vacancies.

This recent period of relatively high unemployment has particularly affected two groups in the labour force: the over-sixties and those in their twenties.

Sources:
Annual Abstract of Statistics
Department of Employment Gazette

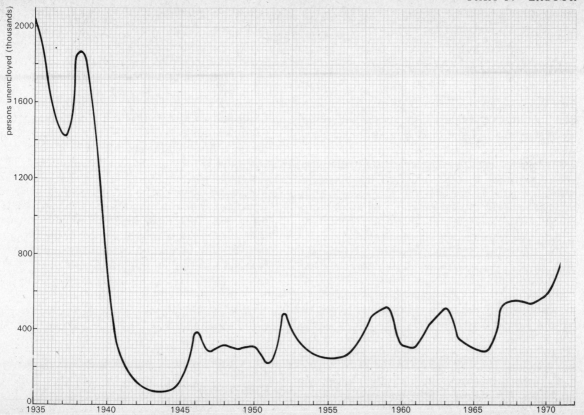

Armed Services

Manpower of army, navy and air force: United Kingdom

Our graph shows the period from the run-down of the armed services which took place after the second world war.

The rapid demobilization of the immediate post-war years was halted in 1950, and for some years the emergency of the Korean war and other armed actions overseas contrived to keep the manpower needs of the services above the 1950 level. The totals for the three services include men locally enlisted abroad.

The Navy relies less upon short-term recruitment than the other two services, and its numbers show less fluctuation in this period.

The post-war period shows the effect of the decision to abandon conscription as a means of providing recruits. Formal conscription has been rare in British history, having been used only during the second half of the first world war and throughout the second world war, although the press gangs in the coastal towns during the Napoleonic wars were in effect a rough and ready form of conscription. Many other countries (e.g.

USSR and USA) have used full or selective conscription to staff their armed forces in peacetime, but since the 1950s Britain has returned to the traditional policy of relying on a volunteer, professional, and highly equipped force.

Post-war recruitment, once conscription was abandoned, has rarely met the estimated manpower needs of the services. These needs are, of course, infinitely lower than war-time requirements. The total strength of the three services, in the peak year of 1945, reached over four and a half million men and women.

Sources:
Defence Statistics
Defence Estimates

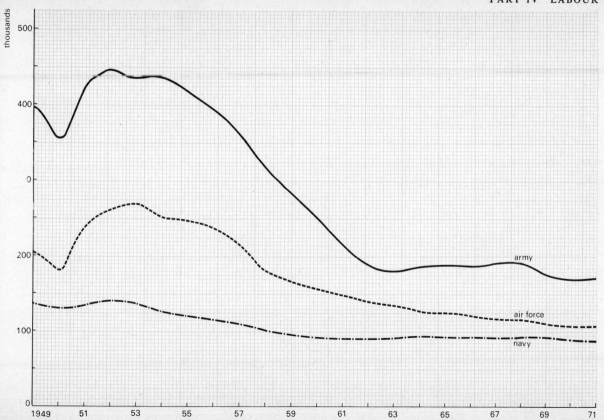

Part V
The Economy

Public expenditure
Private expenditure
Incomes
Taxes
Balance of payments
Exports
Tourism

Public Expenditure

Selected items of expenditure as percentage of GNP: United Kingdom

These percentages have been calculated from the published totals of public spending on seven main items. They show the proportion that this spending comprises of the Gross National Product of the United Kingdom.

Public spending refers to the whole of public expenditure, both government and local authority. It includes current expenditure as well as grants to persons and businesses in the private sector, and expenditure on fixed domestic capital formation.

The graph shows selected items, which are not in all cases the biggest. For example, expenditure on industry and trade, especially in public corporations, now comprises 4·3% of GNP.

Defence includes civil defence. Housing means houses and flats provided by public and local authorities, including New Town corporations, as well as public loans to building societies and housing associations. It does not include private spending on housing.

Education refers to state and local authority spending on schools, colleges, and universities, including grants and scholarships but not the school milk and meals services. Social Security includes the National Insurance scheme, retirement pensions, family allowances, and supplementary benefit. Law Enforcement involves spending on the police, prisons, and the law courts.

It is evident from this graph that increased spending on education, social security, and the health service has been met out of 'savings' in the defence budget. The total sum spent on defence has increased slowly, and now stands at a little under £2,500 million a year, but this represents a massive decline in 'real' expenditure on defence.

Source:
National Income and Expenditure

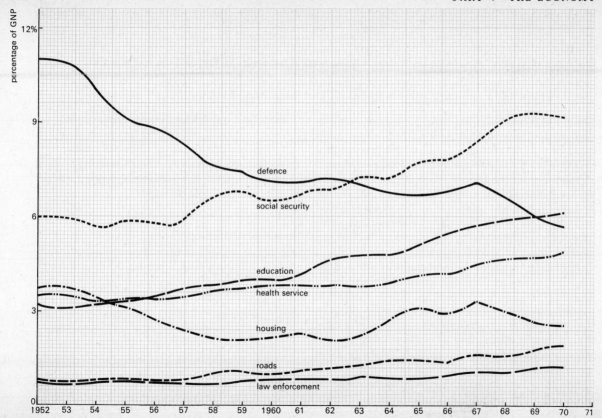

percentage of GNP

12%

9

6

3

defence

social security

education

health service

housing

roads

law enforcement

1952 53 54 55 56 57 58 59 1960 61 62 63 64 65 66 67 68 69 70 71

Expenditure on main services provided: United Kingdom

Spending on education has dominated local authority budgets since the mid 1950s, and it now takes the lion's share of the rates as well as much of the grant money provided to local authorities by the central government.

The totals include current *and* capital expenditure by the local authorities, i.e. spending on staff and salaries as well as on bricks and mortar. The expenditure on roads includes public lighting, and on law and order includes the administration of justice as well as the police forces.

Health includes both the local authority share of the Health Service, and the public health services provided locally. The drop in spending on health from 1948 onwards occurred because of the transfer of some services from the local authorities to the newly created Health Service. The change-over was in 1946, but was not recorded under separate headings in the financial statistics until 1948.

Spending on education does not include scholarships and grants to individuals; these now run at £153 millions a year (1970). Neither does it include spending on school meals and milk (a further £132 million).

The services shown are selected items; other important local authority services include: sewerage and refuse disposal (£400 millions a year), and libraries and museums (£42 millions).

Source:
National Income and Expenditure

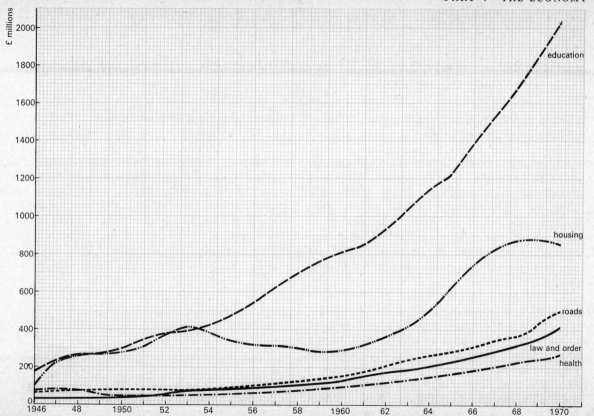

£ millions

education

housing

roads

law and order

health

2000

1800

1600

1400

1200

1000

800

600

400

200

1946   48   1950   52   54   56   58   1960   62   64   66   68   1970

133

Consumers' Expenditure

Consumers' expenditure on selected items: United Kingdom

During a period of growing 'real' incomes, it seems that expenditure on food increases at a faster rate than on any other item of private spending. This is partly true because in a period of growing population the demands for food will rise in a way that is not true of all commodities, especially those not purchased by the young. *Per capita* spending on food has not risen proportionately nearly so much. The expenditure shown is at current prices, and is therefore affected by inflation, but the relationship between the different lines shows the changing *relative* importance of food, housing and so on.

The items shown are selected, and do not cover the entire pattern of consumer spending, but they are the main objects of expenditure with the exception of the running costs of motor vehicles, which in 1970 slightly outstripped the costs of fuel and light. Other items are: household goods other than clothing and durable goods (£910 million in 1970), and books, magazines, and papers (£463 million). These figures are subject to a certain amount of retrospective revision each year, and so do not exactly tally with those published in the first edition of this book.

Housing includes rent, rates, water charges, maintenance repairs, and improvements by occupiers. Clothing includes footwear. Durable goods include motor cars, furniture and carpets, and radio and electrical goods, but not household textiles, soft furnishings, or hardware.

Source:
National Income and Expenditure

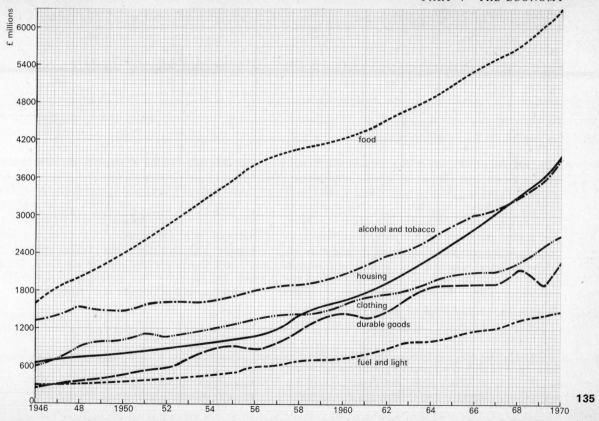

£ millions

6000

5400

4800

4200

food

3600

3000

alcohol and tobacco

2400

housing

1800

clothing

durable goods

1200

fuel and light

600

0

1946   48   1950   52   54   56   58   1960   62   64   66   68   1970

135

Family Spending

Average weekly expenditure per family: Great Britain

The diagram shows the findings of the 1971 Family Expenditure Survey carried out by the Department of Employment.

The average weekly income of a household in Britain includes the earnings not just of the main breadwinner, but working wives, children, etc. Their expenditure, under its main headings, is shown in amounts per week.

The Survey is a continuous sample survey now using over 7,000 households, and has been carried out since 1957. As well as providing a fascinating range of detail and information for government departments, research workers, universities and so on, the findings of the survey are used to calculate the 'weightings' of the different items in the Index of Retail Prices (see page 139); that is, the balance or distribution of people's spending on different items.

Some explanation is needed of the various headings used. Housing includes rent, rates, insurance, but excludes mortgages. Fuel, Light and Power: gas, coke, coal, oil, and electricity. Food: all foodstuffs. Alcoholic Drink: beer, wines, cider, and spirits. Tobacco: cigarettes, pipe tobacco, and cigars. Clothing and Footwear: all shoes and ready-made clothes, and clothing materials including any making-up charges. Durable Household Goods: mainly furniture, electrical goods, appliances, china, cutlery, linen, and furnishings. Other Goods: includes sports goods, medicines, books and papers, animals and pets, matches, cleaning materials, etc. Services: items such as postage, cinemas and theatres, hairdressing, domestic help, educational expenses, medical fees, hotel and holiday spending. Transport and Vehicles: cost of buying and running motor vehicles, as well as bus and train fares.

Source:
Family Expenditure Survey

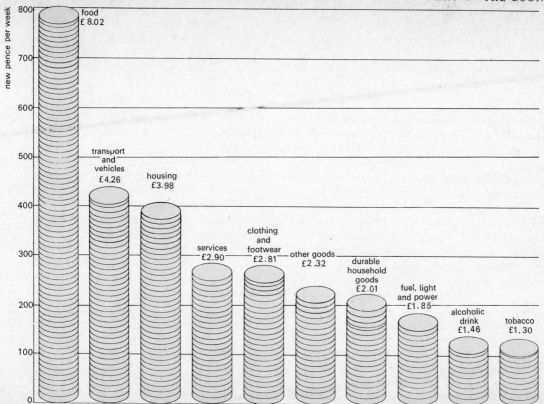

new pence per week

food
£8.02

transport
and
vehicles
£4.26

housing
£3.98

services
£2.90

clothing
and
footwear
£2.81

other goods
£2.32

durable
household
goods
£2.01

fuel, light
and power
£1.85

alcoholic
drink
£1.46

tobacco
£1.30

Prices

Index of retail prices for selected items: United Kingdom

If one wishes to trace changes in the price levels of different commodities over a number of years, to show how one has moved in relation to the others, the technical way of doing this is to construct an *index*. The index of retail prices, illustrated opposite, is commonly called the 'cost of living index'.

A specific year (in this case January of 1956) is selected, and all the prices of the various commodities are regarded as 100. Prices in later years are then expressed as percentage increases or decreases on the prices in that original year. If the price of food in January 1956 was regarded as 100, and it had risen by the end of 1959 by 8·2, the index figure is then 108·2 (see opposite).

Price rises *themselves* are not of great importance; what is important is the impact these rises have on people's budgets. To construct the original index, thirteen thousand households kept records of their expenditure for the then Ministry of Labour, and this evidence was used to construct 'typical' family budgets.

Expenditure on different items was then 'weighted' statistically to allow for its relative importance in family spending.

The result is a continuously moving record, not of the whole cost of living, but at least of that part of it which is affected by retail prices. The items shown opposite are four of the ten main commodity groups used in the index, and are figures for monthly averages in the successive years. The 'weightings' of items were changed in 1962, but the index has been calculated back to 1956 to provide a continuous record. This may cause some very slight inconsistency between pre- and post-1962 figures.

Source:
Department of Employment Gazette

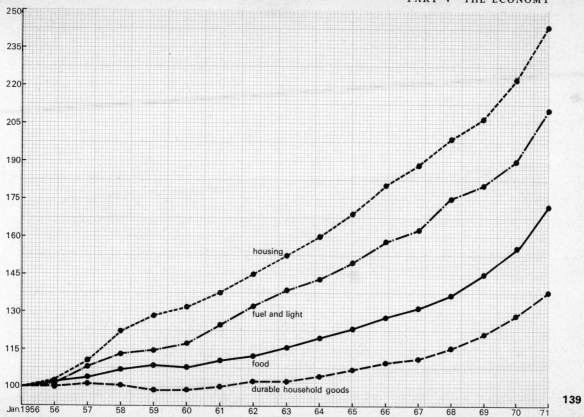

Incomes

Range of personal incomes after tax: United Kingdom

Both through the effect of inflation and (arguably) through the impact of taxation policy, the number of people on low incomes has declined since the 1930s, and the number earning high incomes has risen.

These income-groupings show proportions of tax-payers in different income categories after tax. Company income is not included, and a married couple is counted as one person even if they are assessed separately for tax purposes. All income is included, from employment, self-employment, and from investments or rents.

In addition to normal tax returns, the Inland Revenue has conducted Quinquennial Surveys of personal incomes since 1949, and smaller annual surveys since 1962. Income shown is income *as declared for tax purposes*, and does not include income (e.g. the first £15 of interest on a savings bank deposit) which is exempt from tax.

The 1966–70 returns only start at £330 a year, as that was the effective 'floor' at which incomes became liable to tax.

It would be rash to base any generalizations about greater 'equality' or 'levelling' of income distribution simply upon these figures. Indirect taxation and social security payments must be taken into account; some incomes may be received in ways which render them less liable for tax, and the effects of inflation must also be allowed for.

Sources:
Annual Reports of HM Commissioners of Inland Revenue
Inland Revenue Statistics

140

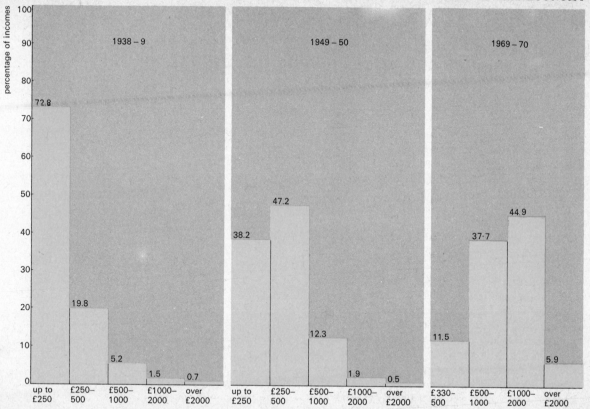

Incomes

Wages, salaries and prices compared: Great Britain

Contrary to popular belief, prices have *not* risen faster than incomes during recent years.

Again, we have an index, this time with the *average* for the year 1955 as 100, and the position at the end of that year and subsequent years plotted in terms of percentage growth for weekly wages, salaries, wage rates, and prices.

Thus the graph shows not the absolute position of wages, salaries etc., but the *relative* extent to which they have risen.

The difference between average weekly earnings and weekly wage rates is that the latter is the official, or *negotiated* weekly wage; in fact people, especially in manufacturing industries, work a good deal of overtime and earn above the basic rates. The gap between these two figures is known by economists as 'wage-drift', and represents the amount by which wages have 'drifted' above their basic level. So 'average weekly earnings' shows what people actually get, and have risen at almost exactly the same rate as salaries since 1955.

Source:
Department of Employment Gazette

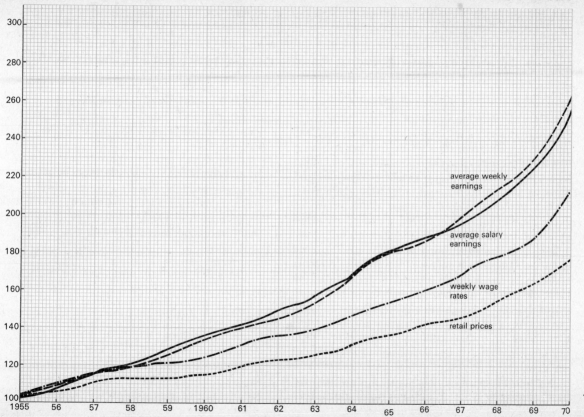

average weekly
earnings

average salary
earnings

weekly wage
rates

retail prices

143

Taxes

Government revenue from taxes on expenditure: United Kingdom

Inflation, plus increases in government spending, has sent the revenue from taxes on expenditure spiralling upwards since the 1930s. The figures refer to the United Kingdom exchequer, and only include Northern Ireland to the extent that taxes are paid to the UK Parliament.

Other similar taxes not shown here include protective duties (£250 millions in 1970), betting tax (£124 millions), and stamp duties (£124 millions).

It is clear from the graph that the heavy reliance upon the smoker as a source of government revenue, although by no means diminished, is now rivalled by taxes on alcohol, and has been surpassed by tax on petrol and oil. Although these items seem to be taxed less heavily than in many European countries, it is nevertheless true that (contrary to common belief) taxes on expenditure in Britain are high by international standards (see page 148).

In years to come, a continuation of this graph would have to take a different form, as from April 1973 Value Added Tax is scheduled to replace Purchase Tax and SET.

In any overall picture of government income, taxes on expenditure as shown here must be set beside all other sources of income, the main ingredients of which are National Insurance contributions (which yielded £2,395 million in 1970), Income Tax (£5,520 million), and Corporation Tax (£1,677 million).

Source:
National Income and Expenditure

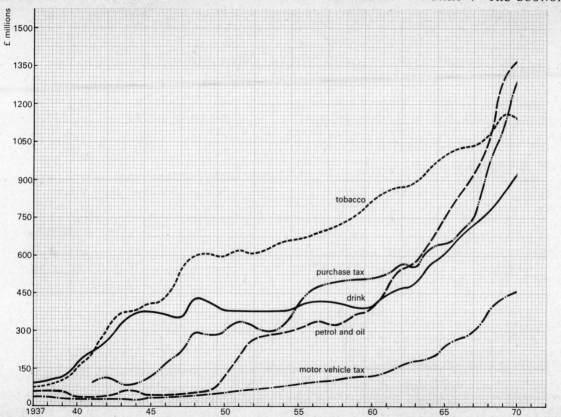

£ millions

tobacco

purchase tax

drink

petrol and oil

motor vehicle tax

1937 40 45 50 55 60 65 70

145

Income Tax

Standard rate in the pound: United Kingdom

Changes in the standard rate of income tax are shown here for this century. The standard rate is not levied upon all one's income, but is the rate of tax paid on income remaining after one's various allowances have been calculated.

Income tax is not a twentieth-century invention. The tax was first introduced by Pitt as a war-time measure in 1799, and was first levied at two shillings in the pound. It obliged all income-earners to make a return of their income, and was predictably unpopular. The tax was repealed in 1802, but restored again the following year until it was again repealed, in 1815, at the end of the Napoleonic war.

Re-introduced by Peel in 1842, income tax has remained ever since, and has become an increasingly important source of government revenue. In a sense, it is still a temporary tax, as it expires every year on 5 April and must be renewed by Parliament.

The high rate of tax during the second world war raised problems of payment which were overcome by the introduction of the PAYE (pay as you earn) scheme in 1944.

From 1966–7 onwards income tax has not been levied on the profits of companies, which now pay the new Corporation Tax. As a tax on incomes, income tax is linked with surtax, which is levied on earned income over £6,300 a year (1971–2), and which yields over £260 million a year. This distinction will vanish, however, when the two rates of tax become part of a unified income tax. Income tax yielded £5,500 millions in 1970.

Source:
Annual Reports of Commissioners of Inland Revenue

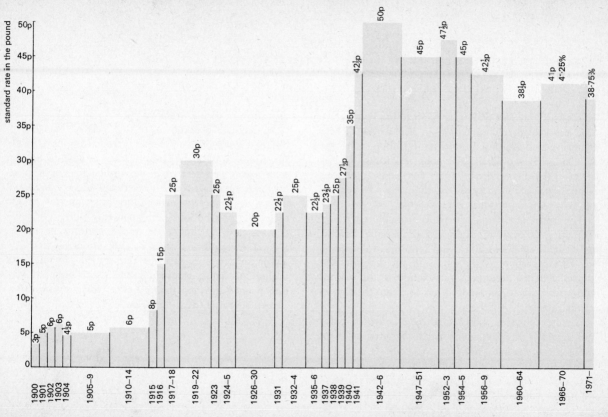

standard rate in the pound

50p
45p
40p
35p
30p
25p
20p
15p
10p
5p
0

1900 3p
1901 5p
1902 6p
1903 6p
1904 4½p
1905–9 5p
1910–14 6p
1915 8p
1916 15p
1917–18 25p
1919–22 30p
1923 25p
1924–5 22½p
1926–30 20p
1931 22½p
1932–4 25p
1935–6 22½p
1937 23½p
1938 25p
1939 27½p
1940 35p
1941 42½p
1942–6 50p
1947–51 45p
1952–3 47½p
1954–5 45p
1956–9 42½p
1960–64 38½p
1965–70 41p 4·25%
1971– 38·75%

Taxation

Taxes as percentage of GNP: International

It is a basic premise of British political life that we are 'the most highly taxed nation in the world'. These figures, which are based upon returns supplied to the OECD by the various member countries, show that this is not so. The figures are for 1969. They show total taxes (including social security contributions) as a percentage of gross national product at factor cost.

This form of calculation avoids 'double counting' by taking taxes as a proportion of national income *before* taxes on expenditure, and subsidies, are counted in. This procedure is the same for all the countries shown, and the definitions of taxation in the various countries have been standardized to make the figures comparable.

All the countries shown here have shown a rising trend, with taxes taking an increasing proportion of GNP during the late 1960s.

Total taxation includes central and local government taxes, both direct and indirect, and the only form of taxation excluded is taxes on capital, which are seen as a form of capital transfer.

A detailed breakdown of the relative weight of different *kinds* of taxes is also provided by the OECD. If we look at different kinds of taxes *as a percentage of total taxes*, we find that in the United Kingdom taxes on households are about average, as are taxes on companies; taxes on expenditure are high, but social security contributions are markedly low. Only in Canada and Denmark do social security payments form a lower proportion of total taxation.

So far as subsidies are concerned, the United Kingdom's figure is now quite high, with only Norway and France showing higher figures for subsidies as a percentage of GNP at factor cost.

Source:
Economic Trends

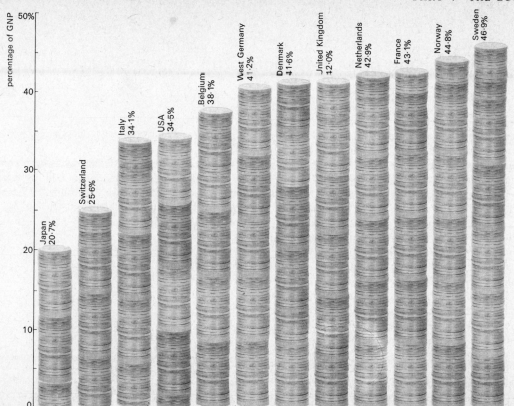

percentage of GNP

50%

40

30

20

10

0

Japan 20·7%
Switzerland 25·6%
Italy 34·1%
USA 34·5%
Belgium 38·1%
West Germany 41·2%
Denmark 41·6%
United Kingdom 42·0%
Netherlands 42·9%
France 43·1%
Norway 44·8%
Sweden 46·9%

Inflation

Annual purchasing power of the pound: United Kingdom

If the purchasing power of a sum of money, taken for the sake of convenience to be one pound sterling, is compared over the period from 1900 to 1971, the resulting changes in its value can be seen from the diagram opposite. The diagram is based upon a series reproduced in Butler and Freeman: *British Political Facts 1900–67*, and was in turn based on a price index calculated by G. Wood in Layton and Crowther: *An Introduction to the Study of Prices* (1938), as well as on Department of Employment cost of living indices and on the post-war consumers' price index.

Inflation has eroded the value of a 1900 pound by a factor of eight times since the beginning of this century. Perhaps the most interesting period shown is the inflation after the first world war. The war ended with the cost of living over 100% higher than it had been in 1914. Demand outran supply, and there was a sharp rise in prices during the boom of 1919–20. The inflation was part of a European trend, and was tackled in Britain by the government's deflationary policies of 1920.

Post second world war inflation has been persistent, and seems to be accepted as a built-in feature of economic life. All post-war governments have made attempts to control it, the latest attempt being the prices and incomes policies.

Source:
Butler, D. and Freeman, J., *British Political Facts 1900–67*

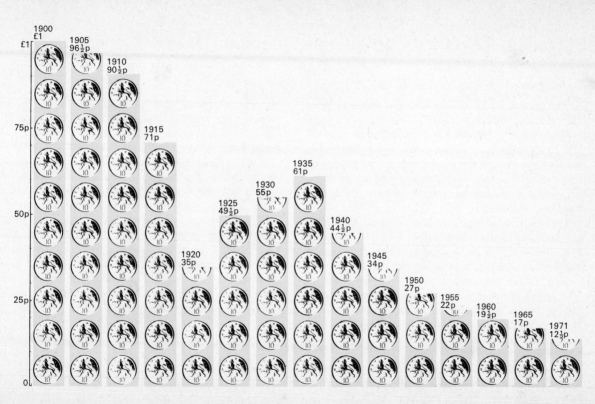

Balance of Payments

Surpluses or deficits on current account: United Kingdom

The balance of payments is a somewhat technical term, and may need some explanation. It represents the gains or losses made in the course of transactions between the United Kingdom and the rest of the world. The figures shown here refer to the *current* balance of payments; this means that *capital* transactions, such as loans between governments or private investment abroad, have been excluded.

The current balance is made up from two main components. Firstly, there is the 'visible' balance of payments, which is the amount by which the value of exports has exceeded imports, or vice versa. These are valued 'f.o.b.' (free on board), which means that the cost of insurance and freight charges has been deducted. On the visible balance of payments, Britain has only been in credit during two periods since the war, in 1956 and 1958, and then again in 1970 and 1971.

Secondly, there is the 'invisible' balance. This consists of items like tourism, profits on investments abroad, diplomatic expenses, and profit earned by shipping, banking, and insurance companies. In this sphere, our economic position is stronger, and the invisible balance has earned a surplus in every year since 1948.

Official figures distinguish between our trading record with sterling area countries, and with the rest of the world. We are normally in balance with the sterling area, and out of balance with non-sterling countries.

The figures opposite are subject to constant revisions, and will not in all cases tally with those previously published. Figures published in the future, similarly, will not necessarily match these exactly.

Strenuous efforts by the government to secure a more favourable balance of payments have clearly shown signs of success in recent years.

Source:
United Kingdom Balance of Payments

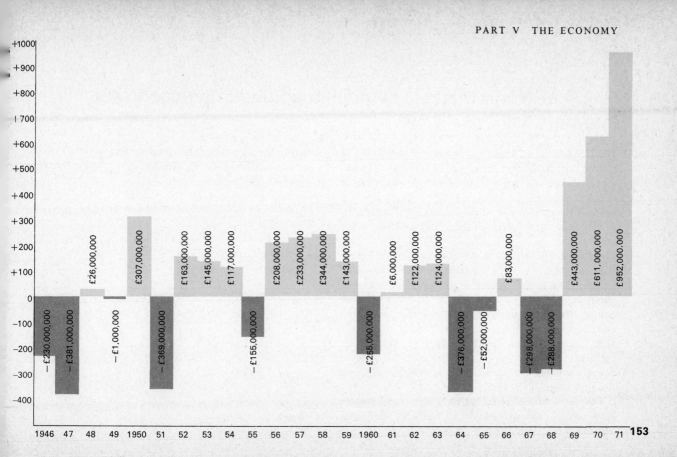

Exports

Share of world markets by main manufacturing countries: International

The Department of Trade and Industry and the OECD collect figures for the value of manufactured goods exported by the main manufacturing countries. A selection of those countries is given opposite, and the value of their exports has been calculated as a percentage share of the total for all the countries listed by the OECD.

A comparison with 1938 would show that the United Kingdom and Germany (at that time the *whole* of Germany) were the leading exporting countries, with about 22% each of world exports of manufactures. Britain emerged from the war with a similar share, but was soon overtaken by the United States. Since then, Germany (now West Germany) has regained the share she had lost during and after the war, the United States has remained a prominent exporting power, and Britain's share of the total has declined.

The share of markets held by Italy, whose figures have almost exactly shadowed those of Belgium–Luxembourg during the last few years, has risen since before the war. Other countries not shown here include Canada (6% in 1971), Sweden (3·3%), Switzerland (2·9%) and the Netherlands (4·6%).

Source:
Trade and Industry

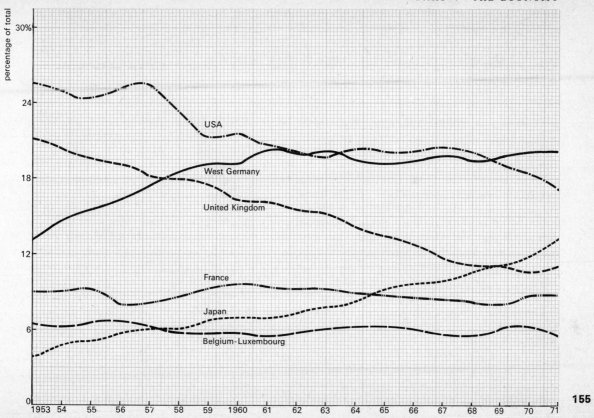

percentage of total

30%

24

18

12

6

0

USA

West Germany

United Kingdom

France

Japan

Belgium-Luxembourg

1953 54   55   56   57   58   59 1960   61   62   63   64   65   66   67   68   69   70   71

Tourism

Number of visits to United Kingdom

In a given year, tourists and other visitors come to Britain from all over the world and we show here the main national contingents, with their relative numbers compared, for the year 1970.

These are totals for *visits*, by overseas residents (technically speaking, persons who are permanently resident elsewhere and who visit the UK for less than twelve months), who come for holidays, business trips, visits to friends and relations, to study, for sporting events, and for health or religious purposes. Roughly half (45%) came for a holiday in 1970, 19% came on business, and 18% came to stay with friends and relations.

These figures include visitors from the Commonwealth, but not those from the Irish Republic, from which an estimated 780,000 people made visits in 1970.

At the end of the second world war the number of tourists totalled a mere 200,000, and the figure has been rising steadily ever since. It topped one million in 1955 and rose to nearly five million in 1968. The newly formed British Tourist Authority, set up with government support and finance, is working towards a target of ten million tourists a year by the mid-1970s.

This growth in tourism brings important economic gains. Britain has always suffered a drain in foreign exchange, through the more than five million people who now take holidays abroad. But in 1968, for the first time, we earned more from foreign visitors than British people spent abroad. Visitors spent £433 million in 1970, and to that sum should be added a further £134 million which they paid to British air and shipping concerns. Altogether, this represents about five pence in every pound of foreign currency earned by the United Kingdom.

Source:
Trade and Industry

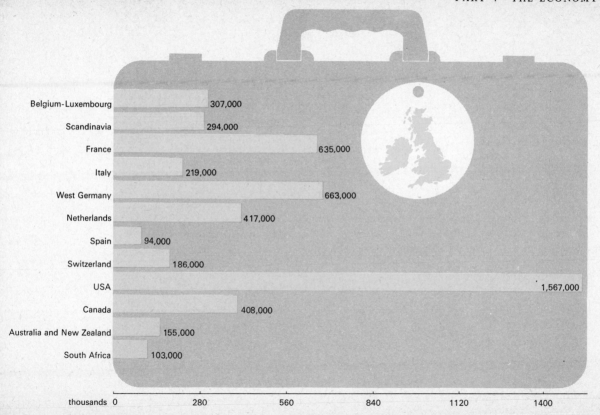

Belgium-Luxembourg	307,000
Scandinavia	294,000
France	635,000
Italy	219,000
West Germany	663,000
Netherlands	417,000
Spain	94,000
Switzerland	186,000
USA	1,567,000
Canada	408,000
Australia and New Zealand	155,000
South Africa	103,000

thousands 0   280   560   840   1120   1400

Part VI
Road Transport

Cars
Highway expenditure
Road accidents

Cars and Motor Cycles

Number of cars and motor cycles in use: United Kingdom

By 1947 the number of cars on the road had already reached the pre-war peak of 1938, and after rising slowly during the late 1940s demand 'took off' in 1952. Since then it has never stopped rising steeply and it is only in the late 1960s and early 1970s that this rapid rate of growth has begun to tail off.

Traffic figures for Northern Ireland as well as for Great Britain are collated by the British Road Federation, from whom these statistics are taken.

The number of goods vehicles has risen more slowly than the number of cars; in 1935 there were approximately half a million goods vehicles on the road, and there are now about one and a half million.

The total for motor cycles includes mopeds, scooters and three-wheelers. The highest figure for this group, in 1961–2, probably represented the peak in the sales of scooters. Motor cycles, like pedal cycles, are a commodity for which demand rises as living standards rise, but only up to a certain point. Beyond that point, they are progressively abandoned as incomes permit people to switch to a more sophisticated form of transport.

Source:
BRF: Basic Road Statistics

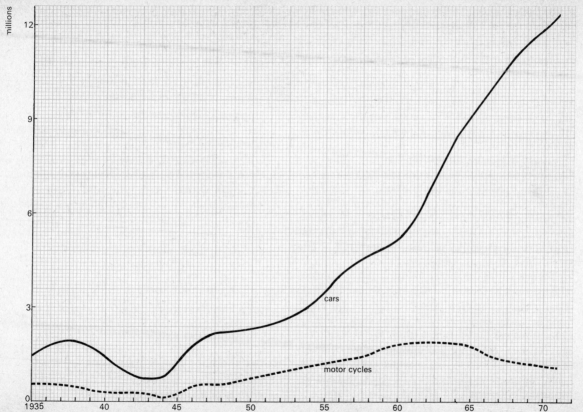

millions

cars

motor cycles

1935   40   45   50   55   60   65   70

161

Motor Cars

Number of persons per car: International

The most effective means of comparing the extent of car ownership between one country and another is to divide the number of cars into the total population. The result is a figure for 'persons per car'. The comparisons are made by the British Road Federation, and are based upon information provided by the International Road Federation.

'Cars' here means motor-cars and taxis, but excludes lorries and commercial vehicles. The figures are for 1970, with the exception of those for Italy, USA, and Switzerland, which are for 1969.

In broad terms, car ownership is related to standard of living, and the countries which are compared here are those whose inhabitants have the highest *per capita* incomes in the world. In India, by contrast, there are 920 persons per car. But there is not an exact relationship between ownership and incomes. Some countries (e.g. USSR) have tended to discourage car production, while others have effectively held back demand by taxing motoring heavily.

Again, in countries which are predominantly rural there is a greater incentive for people to buy cars, as they may represent the only means of transport. In Britain car ownership is high in areas like East Anglia, which do not have especially high *per capita* incomes, but where distances are great and where alternative means of transport are less common than in the cities.

Source:
BRF: Basic Road Statistics

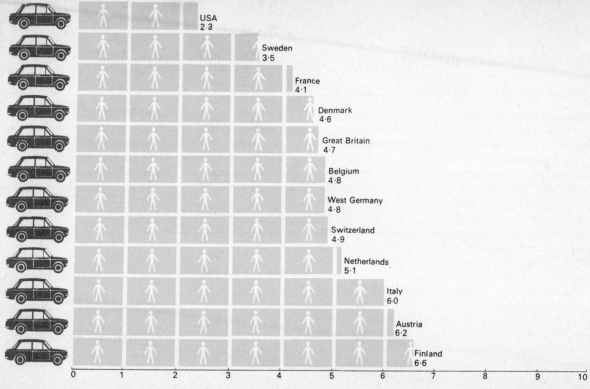

USA
2·3

Sweden
3·5

France
4·1

Denmark
4·6

Great Britain
4·7

Belgium
4·8

West Germany
4·8

Switzerland
4·9

Netherlands
5·1

Italy
6·0

Austria
6·2

Finland
6·6

0 1 2 3 4 5 6 7 8 9 10

persons per car

Roads

Annual expenditure on highways: United Kingdom

Public spending on roads has risen steeply in recent years. The sums shown in the graph include spending on the part of the central government, *and* spending by local authorities. Before the war the local authority share of the total was greater than that for the government; now it is the other way round. Government responsibility for road-building (especially so far as the motorways are concerned) has become steadily greater.

Expenditure on roads includes: construction of new roads; maintenance; repair and improvement; cleansing, watering, and snow clearing; and the administrative costs of trunk roads and other roads.

The total amount of tax received from the motorist, in the form of fuel tax, purchase tax on vehicles, and licence duties, amounted to approximately £1,800 million a year in 1970. Earlier in the century it was assumed that there would be a relationship between motor taxation and the money spent on roads. The Road Fund was set up in 1909 by Lloyd George, to spend motor revenues on road improvements. During the 1920s, however, the Road Fund became used as a source of general government revenue, and since the war motor taxation has been generally viewed as a source of government income to set alongside taxes on drink, tobacco, etc. The Road Fund was formally wound up in 1955.

Source:
BRF: Basic Road Statistics

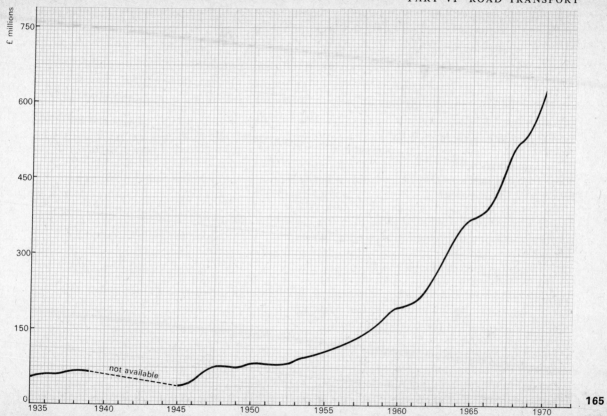

£ millions

750

600

450

300

150

0

not available

1935   1940   1945   1950   1955   1960   1965   1970

Vehicle Density

Vehicles per road mile: International

One important qualification must be made to the term 'vehicles' as it is used here. It includes cars, goods vehicles, buses and coaches, but the International Road Federation (from whom the British Road Federation draw their statistical comparisons) provide no figures for motor cycles or scooters.

The number of vehicles (excluding two-wheelers) is divided into the total number of miles of road in a particular country, and the result is a figure for 'vehicle density'.

An absolutely exact comparison of the relationship between vehicles and road miles is unlikely, as different countries tend to define a 'road' in slightly different ways. A dirt-track highway or country road might be included in the totals for one country, but excluded in another where the totals might be only for made-up roads. So this diagram is able to give no more than a reasonably informative comparison.

The figures are for 1969, and show in each case an increase over previous years. Britain, which already has the highest density of vehicles, has in fact quite a low annual rate of increase (4·7%). By far the highest rate of increase in recent years is recorded by Japan, with an annual growth in density of over 20%.

Source:
BRF: Basic Road Statistics

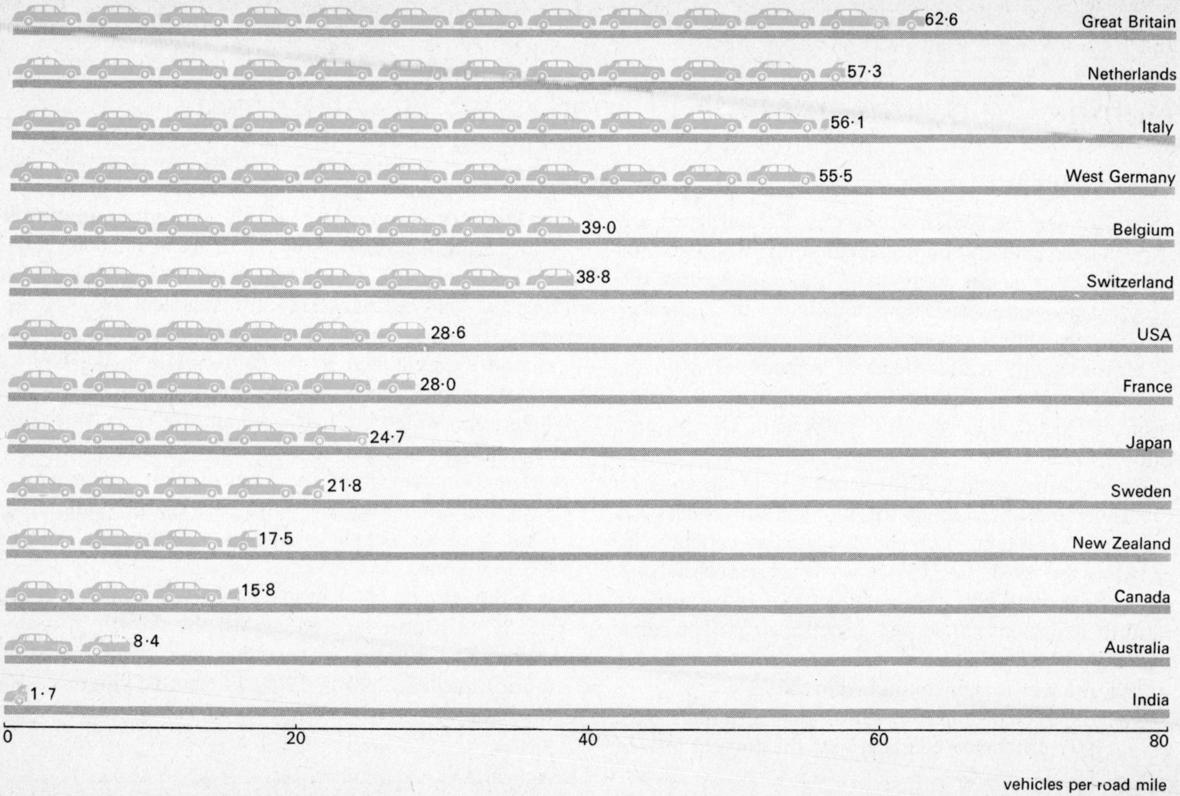

62·6 Great Britain

57·3 Netherlands

56·1 Italy

55·5 West Germany

39·0 Belgium

38·8 Switzerland

28·6 USA

28·0 France

24·7 Japan

21·8 Sweden

17·5 New Zealand

15·8 Canada

8·4 Australia

1·7 India

0 20 40 60 80

vehicles per road mile

Road Accidents

Number of deaths, by type of road user: Great Britain

Death among the four main classes of road users are shown here, and the figures include all deaths except for persons who die more than one month after the accident, in which case they are included in the figures for injured, not for killed.

Motor cyclists include riders of mopeds and scooters and their passengers, and the category of 'other vehicles' includes drivers and passengers of cars and goods vehicles.

The striking feature of the series is that, in spite of the enormous increase in the number of vehicles on the roads, the total number of deaths is roughly the same as for 1935. In 1935 it was motor cyclists and pedestrians who bore the brunt, now it is car drivers (and their passengers) as well as pedestrians. The carnage among pedestrians that accompanied the blackout during the war is shown graphically.

The other change since 1935 is that although road *deaths* have not increased materially, the number *injured* has done so. A quarter of a million were injured each year during the 1930s; now the figure is 350,000.

The number of people killed on the roads since the turn of the century has now reached 335,000, an immense figure although modest compared to the two million lives claimed by the automobile in the United States, a total five times greater than the number of Americans killed in battle in all the wars since the beginning of this century.

The Department of the Environment, using a new basis for calculating the total cost to the community from road accidents, arrived at a figure for 1969 of £320 millions.

Although the total number of road deaths is rising slowly, this must be seen against the growth of motor traffic. The number of casualties per million vehicle-miles travelled (2·90 in 1969) has been falling steadily since the 1950s.

Source:
Annual Abstract of Statistics

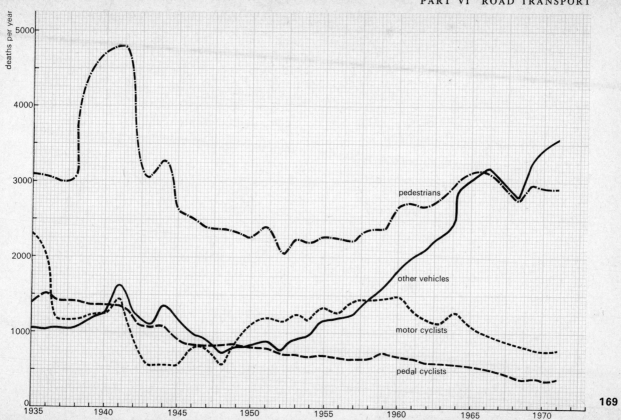

deaths per year

pedestrians

other vehicles

motor cyclists

pedal cyclists

Part VII
Mass Media and Communications

Telephones
Radio and Television
Daily newspapers
Sunday newspapers

Telephones

Persons per telephone: International

This international comparison is made by dividing the total number of telephones in a country into its total population. The figures are for 1969, and are taken from United Nations comparisons, which in turn are derived from the International Telecommunications Union. The method of counting telephones varies slightly from country to country, but not enough to affect the figures materially.

'Telephones' for this purpose means the number of public or private telephones installed which can be connected to a central exchange.

Not surprisingly, perhaps, the country with the fewest persons per telephone (or most telephones per head) is the United States. In general the extent of telephone ownership is related to living standards and to the extent of industrialization. Countries for which UN figures are available, but which are not shown here because the level of ownership is so low, include for example the USSR (20 persons per telephone), Brazil (51), or India (479).

Telephone *usage* (number of calls made per telephone) is reported to be low in Britain. No doubt this is partly due to the fact that we are a densely populated country in which other forms of contact are frequent, and to the fact that we have, by international standards, a very rapid and effective postal system. Unlike some other countries (e.g. USA, Canada) we also make a charge for the cost of local calls.

Source:
United Nations Statistical Yearbook

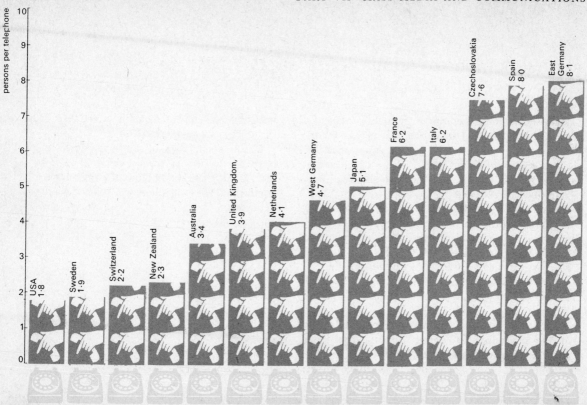

persons per telephone

USA
1·8

Sweden
1·9

Switzerland
2·2

New Zealand
2·3

Australia
3·4

United Kingdom,
3·9

Netherlands
4·1

West Germany
4·7

Japan
5·1

France
6·2

Italy
6·2

Czechoslovakia
7·6

Spain
8·0

East Germany
8·1

Cinema-going

Annual number of admissions: Great Britain

Cinemas make annual returns of the number of their customers, and the total annual number of admissions at the box-office is shown here for the period since the post-war peak in cinema-going. News cinemas are included in the returns, but cinemas showing only 16 mm films are excluded.

The number of admissions is inevitably connected with the decline in the number of cinemas operating commercially. In 1950 there were 4,584 cinemas open; by 1960 this figure had dropped to 3,034, and in 1971 it was down to 1,452, a third of the post-war total.

In 1971 the gross box-office takings were £59 millions, with an average box-office admission price of 82p.

A regional analysis of cinema-going in 1971 reveals that the percentage of seating capacity filled was highest in the South-west (22·1%), followed by the East Midlands (21·9%). The lowest percentage was in Greater London (16·5%). This calculation is based upon the number of complete performances during one week in November, including children's films but excluding news cinemas.

The total number of films registered in Britain continues to decline, from over 1,000 in 1961 to 652 in 1971. Of these the number of British films was 278, comprising 96 long films, 78 short films, and 104 newsreels.

Sources:
Trade and Industry
Annual Abstract of Statistics

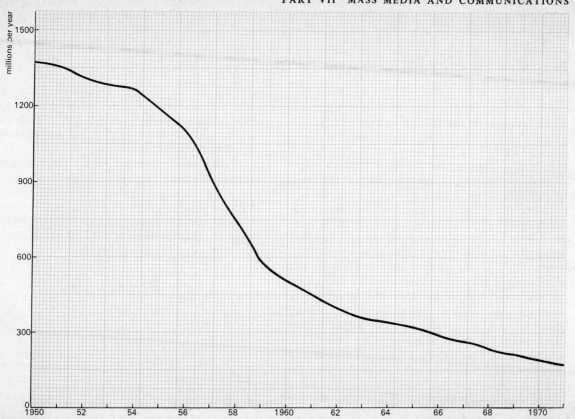

millions per year

Radio and Television

Number of current licences: United Kingdom

Radio broadcasting was first provided in Britain by a commercial concern, the British Broadcasting Company, in 1922. Four years later, in 1926, the British Broadcasting Corporation was established by royal charter, and the new BBC operated from the beginning of 1927. The charter is renewable every ten years.

In 1936 the service was augmented by the first public television programmes, broadcast by the BBC from Alexandra Palace. No television service was provided during the war years, from 1939 to 1946.

After the war, in 1954, legislation permitted the establishment of the first commercial TV companies. Listeners and viewers, of either BBC or ITV programmes, must pay for a receiving licence, and we show opposite the changing number of these licences since 1935. The radio licence was for radio only, whereas the TV licence is a joint one, for radio and TV. From 1971 a separate radio licence has not been required.

The original radio licence fee in 1922 was ten shillings. It was raised to one pound in 1946, and to twenty-five shillings in 1965. The current licence fee of £7 (£12 colour) is still one of the lowest in the world.

All the licence money goes to the BBC, less about four million pounds retained by the Post Office for the costs of collection, etc. The BBC also receives about ten millions a year, as a grant-in-aid, from the Government, for the expenses of running the BBC external services. Approximately two thirds of BBC income is spent on television, and the remainder on radio.

Sources:
Post Office Reports and Accounts
BBC Handbook

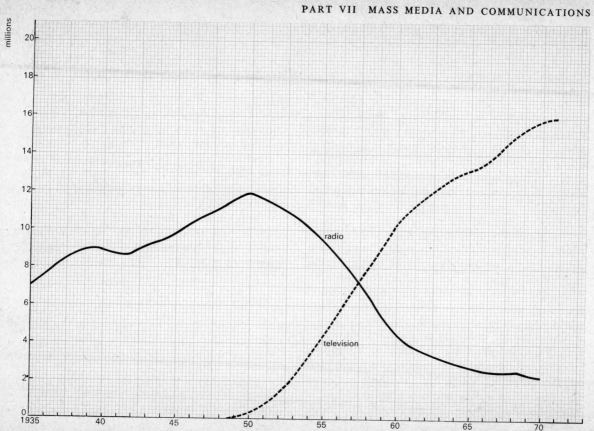

millions

radio

television

1935 40 45 50 55 60 65 70

Daily Newspapers

Sales of 'mass-circulation' newspapers: United Kingdom

The distinction between 'mass-circulation' and 'quality' newspapers is subjective and somewhat invidious, but its use here is defended on the grounds that the 1962 Royal Commission on the Press thought it worth making the distinction, and because it permits circulation comparisons which would lose much of their point if all drawn to the same scale.

The newspapers compared here are London daily morning papers, and include only those currently being published. The only exceptions (apart from the trade and sporting press) are the *Sketch*, and the *Morning Star* (ex-*Daily Worker*) which publishes circulation figures for recent years but not for the whole of the period from 1946 to the present.

Figures are for average net sales, per publishing day, for the second half of the year (July to December). Careful watch is kept on newspaper circulations, both by their publishers and by the advertising world, as sales figures help to determine advertising rates.

A comparison between papers currently in publication inevitably omits many illustrious names from the roll-call of Fleet Street in the post-war period. The *News Chronicle* (itself incorporating the old *Daily News*) was swallowed whole by the *Daily Mail* in 1960, with a noticeable (but evidently temporary) effect on the *Mail's* circulation. The *Daily Herald* has changed its name as well as its character in becoming, in 1964, the *Sun*. The old *Daily Graphic* became the *Daily Sketch* (which we do show in the graph), which in turn ceased publishing in 1971 and merged with the *Daily Mail*.

Source:
Audit Bureau of Circulation

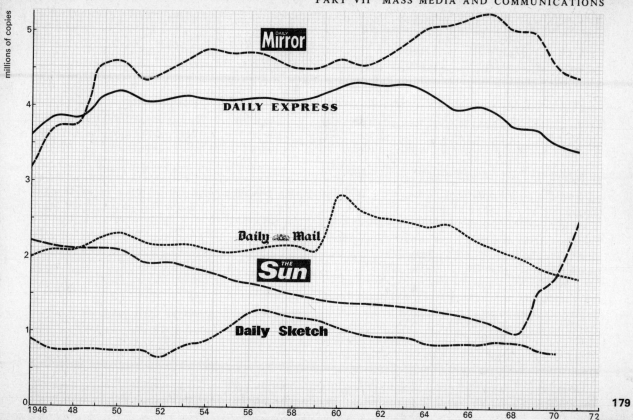

millions of copies

Daily Newspapers

Sales of 'quality' press: United Kingdom

Change in the circulation of these four newspapers is rarely dramatic or sudden, although the rise (and fall) in sales of *The Times* since 1965 is clearly visible.

As in the case of the mass circulation dailies already illustrated, the figures are for average net sales per publishing day during the second half of the year. Sales should not be confused with *readership*; on average, about three people read each copy of a newspaper sold.

Each of these newspapers had a publishing history long before the period we have selected. *The Times* was founded in 1785 as the *Daily Universal Register*, and it has been in private ownership but with a Trust consisting of the Lord Chief Justice, the President of the Royal Society, the Governor of the Bank of England, the President of the Institute of Chartered Accountants, and the Warden of All Souls! In 1966 the paper was bought by the Thomson Organisation, publishers of the *Sunday Times*.

The *Daily Telegraph* dates from 1855, and absorbed the *Morning Post* in 1937.

The *Financial Times* (founded 1888) incorporated the *Financial News* in 1945, and has succeeded since then in more than doubling its circulation.

The *Guardian* (1821) which shows a similar growth in sales, belongs to the Manchester Guardian and Evening News Ltd, and severed some of its connections with Manchester when it became simply the *Guardian* in 1959.

Source:
Audit Bureau of Circulation

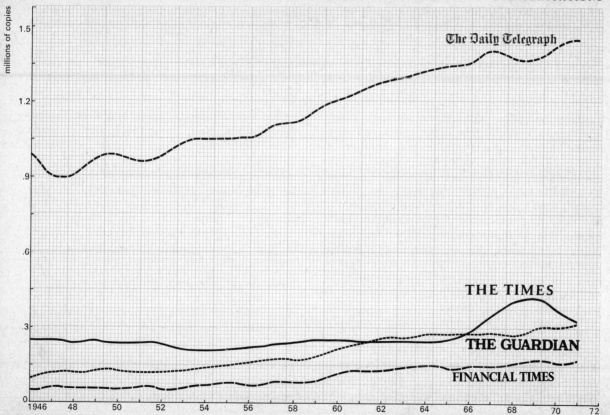

Sunday Newspapers

Sales of Sunday newspapers: United Kingdom

Sunday publishing has been a graveyard of newspapers since the end of the war. The graph shows papers being currently published, and in doing so omits the following papers: *Reynolds News*, which was published by the co-operative movement, became the *Sunday Citizen* in 1962, and ceased publication in 1967. The *Sunday Graphic*, which was once called the *Sunday Herald*, and dates from 1927; it ceased to appear in 1960. *Empire News*, which was swallowed by the *News of the World* in 1960. *Sunday Dispatch*, at one time the *Weekly Dispatch*, but then taken over by the *Sunday Express* in 1961. Lastly the *Sunday Pictorial*, which was absorbed in 1961 by the International Publishing Corporation and renamed the *Sunday Mirror*.

The decade 1960–70 has seen a steady decline in the circulations of the mass circulation Sundays, a decline which, for the *News of the World*, had been in progress since 1950. This decline is matched, during the same period, by the growth of the *Observer* and the *Sunday Times*, and with the appearance of the *Sunday Telegraph*.

As a result of these changes, it became possible during the 1960s to discern a rise in the 'serious' press and a decline in the 'popular' press, a picture which seemed to be true of daily as well as Sunday journalism. However, this picture has been falsified by the phenomenal rise in the fortunes of the *Sun* since 1968.

Source:
Audit Bureau of Circulation

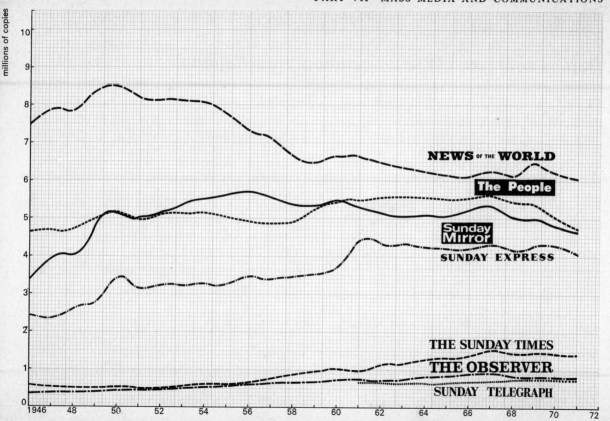

millions of copies

NEWS OF THE WORLD

The People

Sunday Mirror

SUNDAY EXPRESS

THE SUNDAY TIMES

THE OBSERVER

SUNDAY TELEGRAPH

10
9
8
7
6
5
4
3
2
1
0

1946 48 50 52 54 56 58 60 62 64 66 68 70 72

183

Newspaper Readership

Copies sold per 1,000 population: International

The figures are for 1969, and in a few cases for 1968. They refer to *daily* newspapers, and compare the number of copies circulated per thousand population, thus giving a comparison of the extent of newspaper readership which allows for the different population size of different countries.

A daily newspaper is defined by UNESCO for the purposes of these comparisons as a publication containing general news, and appearing at least four times a week. The figures for total circulation include copies sold outside as well as inside the country. In fact, there are few newspapers for which the foreign circulation is an important part of total sales, and, although no allowance is made in the comparisons for foreign sales, it is unlikely that this would affect the figures materially.

Circulation should not be confused with readership, which normally exceeds circulation by a factor dependent upon incomes, family size, readership interest and so on. In Britain, it is estimated that about three people read each copy of a newspaper sold.

It should be borne in mind that the *size* of a daily paper may range from a double sheet to an edition of fifty or more pages. No doubt newspaper circulation is roughly determined by levels of literacy, but that countries with similar levels of literacy can still have widely varying extents of newspaper circulation is evident from these figures. Very low levels of readership, not shown in the diagram, include India (13), Iran (15), and Morocco (14), although these are not the lowest levels recorded.

Source:
United Nations Statistical Yearbook

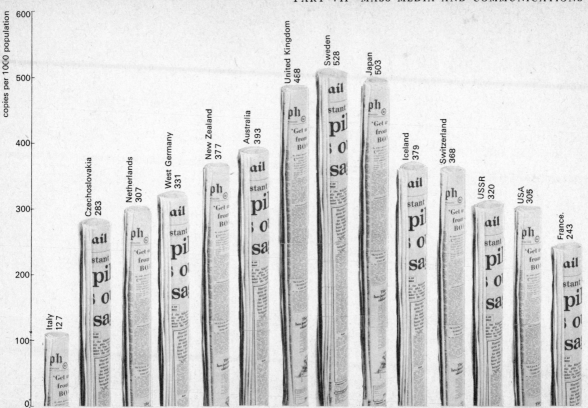

copies per 1000 population

Italy 127
Czechoslovakia 283
Netherlands 307
West Germany 331
New Zealand 377
Australia 393
United Kingdom 488
Sweden 528
Japan 503
Iceland 379
Switzerland 368
USSR 320
USA 305
France 243

Bibliography

B. R. Mitchell and P. Deane: *Abstract of British Historical Statistics*
B. Marlow: *Charting the British Economy*
D. Butler and J. Freeman: *British Political Facts 1900–67*

GOVERNMENT PUBLICATIONS

HMSO: *Britain: An Official Handbook* (annual)
General Register Office: *Census Reports; Annual Statistical Review*
Central Statistical Office: *Annual Abstract of Statistics; Social Trends* (annual); *Monthly Digest of Statistics; Financial Statistics* (monthly); *Economic Trends* (monthly); *National Income and Expenditure* (annual)
Scottish Statistical Office: *Digest of Scottish Statistics*
Welsh Office: *Digest of Welsh Statistics*
Department of Employment: *Gazette* (monthly); *Trade and Industry* (weekly)
Home Office: *Criminal Statistics* (annual)
Dept. of Education and Science: *Statistics of Education* (annual)
Board of Inland Revenue: *Inland Revenue Statistics* (annual)

Department of the Environment: *Highway Statistics* (annual); *Housing Statistics*

INTERNATIONAL

United Nations: *Demographic Yearbook; Statistical Yearbook*
OECD: *Historical Statistics*
International Labour Office: *Yearbook of Labour Statistics*

More about Penguins and Pelicans

Penguinews, which appears every month, contains details of all the new books issued by Penguins as they are published. From time to time it is supplemented by *Penguins in Print*, which is a complete list of all available books published by Penguins. (There are well over four thousand of these.)

A specimen copy of *Penguinews* will be sent to you free on request. For a year's issues (including the complete lists) please send 30p if you live in the United Kingdom, or 60p if you live elsewhere. Just write to Dept EP, Penguin Books Ltd, Harmondsworth, Middlesex, enclosing a cheque or postal order, and your name will be added to the mailing list.

Note: *Penguinews* and *Penguins in Print* are not available in the U.S.A. or Canada

Penguin Reference Books

Facts in Focus

Compiled by the Central Statistical Office

Statistics are a part of our way of life. Almost everyone uses them either to make points in discussion or as a basis for taking decisions. Politicians argue over them, businessmen and administrators plan with them, trade unionists bargain around them.

This reference book of statistical tables and charts has been prepared by the Government Statistical Service. It contains the essential figures and indicates trends in a great variety of areas of public concern in Britain:

The economy (public and private expenditure, taxation, savings, investment)

Education (schools, universities, expenditure)

Industry and trade (manufacturing and service industries, distribution exports)

Manpower (employment and unemployment, wages, strikes)

Population (births, marriages, deaths, ages, density, migration)

Social services (housing, welfare, health, law and order)

How to Lie with Statistics

Darrell Huff

'Round numbers,' pronounced Dr Johnson, 'are always false.'

But not, of course, the precise and scientific calculations of trained statisticians, with their decimals and percentages. The computer, like the camera, cannot lie. Not without help, anyhow.

In this Pelican Darrell Huff introduces the beginner to the niceties of samples (random or stratified random), averages (mean, median, or modal), errors (probable, standard, or unintentional), graphs, indexes and other tools of democratic persuasion.

John Connell, in the *Evening News*, called this famous study 'wildly funny, outrageous, and a splendid piece of blasphemy against the preposterous religion of our time'.

But don't let that depress you. Figures prove that there's always something to weep about – whether it's cancer, the cost of living, crime, or just the Chinese population. Yes, more and more people are dying every day. It's the trend.